A Survival Guide
in the Information Age
145 Important Tips to Protect You and Your Family

D1506585

Also by Derek Smith

Risk Revolution

A Survival Guide
in the Information Age
145 Important Tips to Protect You and Your Family

Derek Smith

LONGSTREET PRESS

Published by
Longstreet Press, Inc.
2974 Hardman Court
Atlanta, Georgia 30305

Copyright © 2004 by ChoicePoint Asset Company

1st printing, 2004

ISBN: 1-56352-737-5

Printed in the United States of America

Book design by Bright Impact, Inc.

Contents

Acknowledgements

In the process of writing this book, I have learned that publishing is a team effort. And, the members of the team who have helped take this book from concept to reality deserve to be recognized.

First, Steve Chamberlain. It was his energy and encouragement that convinced me to write this book. A former executive at Turner Broadcasting and WebMD, Steve has long been a leader in the effort to empower consumers with the information they need to make good decisions.

I also want to thank the ChoicePoint associates who provided valuable information and are helping to bring the positive power of information to individuals: Richard Collier, Michael de Janes, Gloria Griessman, Dr. Kevin McElfresh, Baxter Gillespie, James E. Lee, Deslie Webb Quinby, Michael Reene, Lauren Waits, Leah Williamson and Henri Wiggins.

You would be staring at blank pages were it not for Michele Mitchell and her support team of David Bernknopf and Bobbie Battista at Atamira. This trio interviewed, researched, edited and worked tirelessly to turn my thoughts and words into the book you hold in your hand.

But stark words on a page wouldn't be particularly interesting without the design expertise of Judy Fergusson and her team at Bright Impact. Late nights and last minute changes did not deter this creative group of people from producing an appealing layout that helps drive the message home.

Scott Bard at Longstreet Press has taken two leaps of faith this year by publishing this book and a longer, more detailed book that explores in depth the philosophies we touch on briefly here. I am truly grateful for your help and belief that the responsible use of information will make our world a safer place.

Finally, allow me to thank my family — wife Lisa, daughter Hanley, son Tanner and my parents Dr. and Mrs. D.L. Smith. I am lifted up by your love, support and constant encouragement for my passion to create a safer world for all our generations.

Foreword

It's no cliché to say the world is a riskier place. Riskier in which to live, work, do business and raise your family. The question is, whose job is it to address the variety of risks we face each day?

In a simpler time, we didn't have to worry about many risks. Those we did face were usually taken care of by someone else, oftentimes a government official or someone in authority like a minister or police officer.

Today, you and I are increasingly responsible for ensuring our families are safe, but knowing what to do and how to do it can be a daunting task.

That's why I've written this book. To give you some very practical advice on how to use the latest technologies and information tools to help add some peace of mind to your life.

You can use this book in several ways.

> **It's a handbook.** Each section of the book is designed to help you understand many of the important issues facing individuals and families that are related to the use of information or technology. From identity theft and keeping your children safe online to protecting your investments and your health, each chapter is filled with practical advice.

> **It's a resource guide.** Each chapter includes a list of sources for additional information, products and services that you can use to address the issues of most importance to you.

> **It's a discussion guide.** The concept that each person is now responsible in some way for their own safety and security is one that requires each family member to understand their new role. This book gives you the framework to have a discussion about how your family is going to act on the issues raised in the chapters.

No single book can claim to contain all the answers. Anyone who has ever purchased a car or home computer knows the minute you buy one, there's already a newer, faster (and maybe cheaper) model already in the works. The same is true with the issues addressed in the pages that follow. Every moment, a new twist in technology is developed and, with it, the potential for something good and bad. This guide will help you navigate the ever-changing world of technology and harness the positive power of information to make your personal world a safer place.

A Survival Guide
in the Information Age
145 Important Tips to Protect You and Your Family

CHAPTER 1: **Identity Theft**
When Good Names Go Bad

Michael Berry found out his identity had been stolen in a usual way: he was trying to consolidate his debts onto one low-interest credit card but, to his surprise, he was rejected. A bank clerk apologized, saying, "You have opened too many cards lately." At least fifteen new cards, to be exact.

Berry did not panic. He is in politics; he knows mistakes can be smoothed over. He made the necessary phone calls to the three credit bureaus — Equifax, Experian and TransUnion — and when he received his reports, he began to get very worried. The agencies recorded that he had obtained instant credit from Gap and Old Navy and had used thousands of dollars worth of this credit; he had maxed out a $1,500 limit from the QVC shopping channel; he had charged hundreds of dollars in gas at Exxon stations around Los Angeles; and he had nearly $500 on a new phone line in Riverside, Calif. And, evidently, he had been ardently courting two women with hundreds of dollars in roses and a stuffed bear.

But then, he found out he was wanted for murder.

"I was terrified," Berry says. "There was tremendous confusion over who the 'real' Michael Berry was, and I was

warned that a routine traffic stop could be 'very bad for you'.

The thirty-four year old is the chief operating officer of the Independent Women's Forum, a conservative women's group. He flies around the country, rubbing shoulders with the political elite and Republican activists. And suddenly, his credit rating was ruined and friends were calling him to say, "Hey! You were just the lead story on 'America's Most Wanted'!"

"That scared me to death," Berry says.

Theft of one's identity in order to commit a violent crime is scary enough without even factoring in any money that has been lost. It is as if Hollywood movies foretold the future: think of "The Net," with Sandra Bullock fighting identity snatchers who have criminalized her, or even "Enemy of the State," with Will Smith, whose mistaken identity leads to the NSA mercilessly tracking him. It makes for great entertainment because, well, it *seems* like it couldn't *really* happen.

What Is Identity Theft?

There are four types of identity theft and two types of identity fraud that you should know about.

ID Theft 1: Account Takeover

This is where you steal someone's identity for quick access to existing accounts. When this happens, a thief acquires your *existing* credit account information and purchases products and services using either the actual credit card or just the account number and expiration date. Victims often learn their account has been taken over when they receive their monthly billing statement.

ID Theft 2: Account Theft

This occurs when your ID is stolen and used to take possession of an existing account by changing the address of record. ID thieves may also remove mail from home mailboxes to obtain the information needed to change the address on credit card and bank accounts. When this occurs, victims most often learn of the theft when contacted by their financial institution about the address change, when a credit card is declined (because someone else has run-up the balance) or when they don't receive a monthly statement.

ID Theft 3: Application Fraud

ID thieves can create new accounts through a stolen identity. Application fraud is what some experts call "true name fraud." The thief uses your Social Security Number and other identifying information to open *new* accounts in your name. Victims of application fraud usually aren't aware of it for a while because the monthly account statements are mailed to an address used by the imposter. Awareness of the theft comes when a collection company calls about unpaid accounts or when applications for new credit are rejected because of too many debts.

ID Theft 4: Identity Assumption

The worst form of ID theft occurs when your identity is stolen and the thief becomes you for a period of time (while possibly committing all manner of crimes). Here, your attributes, background, accomplishments or rights and privileges are taken by someone who pretends to be you. A very common trick used by identity thieves is to obtain a fake driver's license with your characteristics and their photo. Victims of ID assumption often find out about the theft when law enforcement officers contact them about crimes they (the ID theft victims) are suspected of committing.

What Is Identity Fraud?

As bad as identity theft is, the two forms of identity fraud may be, in some respects, worse because they are often difficult to discover.

ID Fraud 1: Creating a Fictional Past

People who commit ID fraud often use their real names, but create a fictional resumé that makes them appear to be someone they are not. It could be as innocent as claiming to have a college degree when they don't, to as serious as faking a professional credential. In any event, ID fraud is used to create a person more credible than they are.

ID Fraud 2: Creating a New, Fictional Person

This is the ultimate lie. When you steal someone's identity, each time you use the fake ID you increase the likelihood of being caught. But here, with a manufactured person, the longer you use the fictional persona, the more legitimate you become. However, a thorough background check would reveal that you didn't exist before the date your new personality was "born," a red flag to anyone looking into your credentials.

How Identities Are Stolen

All types of identity theft are pathetically easy and happen all the time. Identity theft is the top consumer fraud in the United States, according to the government agency responsible for responding to ID theft. And it isn't cheap. In the latest statistics, the Federal Trade Commission estimates that identity theft costs consumers and businesses $53 billion annually.

In a recent study, Gartner Inc., a business research group, estimated that 7 million Americans have fallen prey to identity thieves.[1] Star Systems, a company that facilitates the majority of U.S. ATM transactions, did its own study that suggests that almost 12 million Americans in all, or about one in 19 adults, have been hit by such fraud.[2]

Generally, victims of credit and banking fraud are liable for no more than the first $50 of the loss. In many cases, the victim will not be required to pay any part of the loss. But shouldering the bill for identity theft costs Visa and MasterCard, the two major credit card companies, well over $100 million a year.

Did You Know?

- Identity theft is the top consumer fraud in the United States, according to the government agency responsible for responding to ID theft.

- The Federal Trade Commission estimates that identity theft costs consumers and businesses $53 billion annually.

- About one in 19 adults have been hit by such fraud.

- The bill for identity theft costs Visa and MasterCard, the two major credit card companies, well over $100 million a year.

So how do ID thieves do it?

> Identity thieves steal wallets and purses containing your identification and credit and bankcards.

> They steal your mail, including your bank and credit card statements, pre-approved credit offers, telephone calling cards and tax information.

> They rummage through your trash, or the trash of businesses, for personal data in a practice known as "dumpster diving."

> They "shoulder surf" at ATM machines and phone booths in order to capture PIN numbers.

> They fraudulently obtain your credit report by posing as a landlord, employer or someone else who may have a legitimate need for — and a legal right to — the information.

> They get your business or personnel records at work.

> They find personal information in your home.

> They use personal information you share on the Internet.

> They buy your personal information from "inside" sources. For example, an identity thief may pay a store employee for information about you that appears on an application for goods, services or credit.

Armed with this information, several things are possible. Depending upon the thief's intent, each type of identity theft or fraud carries increasing risk.

If you are lucky, the criminal only makes a few quick purchases and abandons your identity like a thief in the night. This is **ID Theft 1**.

If you are not so lucky, identity thieves can use your personal information by calling your credit card issuer and, pretending to be you, ask to change the mailing address on your credit card account. Or, they can take stolen mail and fill out a change of address form.

The imposter then runs up charges on your account. Because your bills are being sent to the new address, it may take some time before you realize there's a problem. Most likely, you'll only discover the problem when you try to use your credit card (but can't because you're "maxed" out) or apply for new credit and you're rejected. This is **ID Theft 2**.

They can also open a new credit card account using your name, date of birth and Social Security number (SSN). When they use the credit card and don't pay the bills, the delinquent account is reported on your credit report.

They may establish phone or wireless service in your name. They may open a bank account in your name and write bad checks on that account. They may file for bankruptcy under your name to avoid paying debts they've incurred or to avoid eviction. They may counterfeit checks or debit cards and drain your bank account. They may buy cars by taking out auto loans in your name. This is **ID Theft 3**.

And sometimes, if they have actually *become* you, they commit murder and the police start looking for *you*. This is **ID Theft 4**.

Demorris Andy Hunter, who stole Michael Berry's name, is a convicted killer who spent 13 years in Folsom State Prison for a 1985 murder. With a California driver's license with Berry's name and Hunter's photo and a fake Social Security card with Berry's number, Hunter moved to Florida, got a job and set up a life. And then he strangled his neighbor to death. It didn't take long for investigating detectives to find their man: Michael Berry.

Meanwhile, the real Michael Berry was struggling with a welter of problems. He tracked his financial problems to an address in Los Angeles and tried to report his situation to L.A. police. But he wasn't a resident and the fraud was not considered large enough, so the police told him there was nothing they could do. Next, Berry called his local police department in Virginia, where a sympathetic officer took his report, but warned that Virginia had no jurisdiction in California.

Then came the call from a Florida homicide detective that a man using his persona was a convicted murderer wanted for new killings in two states. Florida officials figured most of it out. They knew they were looking for a short African American guy; the records they received showed a tall white guy. And from there, detectives pieced together evidence to learn Hunter's real identity. And then they called the real Michael Berry in Virginia to inform him they were about to issue a national warrant for Hunter on murder charges, and that they would use Berry's name as his alias. This meant that the real Michael Berry could be taken into custody as a wanted man at any time.

"Up until that point, I just had to laugh a couple of times at what was happening to me," Berry says. "But then I became genuinely scared that I would be arrested. What if I was pulled over and the police ran my license plate through their system?"

That is exactly how police captured the man who had stolen the identity of a distinguished U.S. military officer.

John M. Harrison is a forty-two year old retired Army Captain who was enjoying his life as a father and salesperson in Rocky Hill, a picturesque small town in Connecticut, when he got a call from a Texas detective regarding a Harley-Davidson that had been purchased under his name — and SSN (Harley had called the police when the $2,700 check used for a deposit on the $25,000 motorcycle bounced). Harrison, the detective told him, was a victim of identity theft.

Harrison did everything right: he reported his situation to the FTC and the credit bureaus, initiated fraud alerts, began contacting creditors, and filed police reports. Just one month later, Jerry Wayne Phillips was arrested in North Carolina on the Harley-Davidson. Phillips pled guilty to one count of identity theft and currently is serving a 41-month sentence in Minnesota.

Easy to fix, right?

Harrison is still suffering from the damage. He had excellent credit history, which allowed Phillips to have a grand old time. Phillips' six-month spending spree included the motorcycle, a Ford pickup and Excursion (financed through Ford Credit), more than 60 accounts at places like Wal-Mart, Home Depot and Lowes, personal and auto loans, four checking accounts and two savings accounts (as far south as Florida, as far north as Virginia and as far west as Texas), utilities, cell phone service, a time-share in South Carolina, and a rental house in Virginia. The grand total, in Harrison's name, was over $260,000.

One of the fraudulent accounts was with the Army & Air Force Exchange Service (AAFES). In March 2002, nearly four months after Phillips was caught and sentenced, the AAFES attempted to garnish Harrison's military retirement pay, twice. The second attempt was successful, and the Army began withholding his retirement checks. It took the aid of a member of Congress to get his retirement reinstated.

> Sometimes you, as an individual, have done nothing wrong. Someone with access to your information has allowed it to be stolen. But you still have primary responsibility for cleaning up the mess.

"The fact that the Army gave away my identity in the first place adds insult to injury," Harrison says. A year and a half after Harrison retired — on July 27, 2001 — Phillips gained control of Harrison's identity when Army officials at Fort Bragg, N.C., issued him an active duty military ID card in Harrison's name, which contained his SSN. Harrison isn't sure how or why the Army issued the identity card to Phillips; he only knows that Phillips said it was "easy."

Harrison's case shows that sometimes you, as an individual, have done nothing wrong. Someone with access to your information has allowed it to be stolen. But you still have primary responsibility for cleaning up the mess.

"I compare it to being blindfolded and stuck in a ring with Mike Tyson," says Harrison, "You have no idea what's out there until it hits you."

Some places that opened accounts on behalf of Harrison's imposter never saw the fraud alert Harrison placed on the credit report in November 2001 (a spokesman for the credit reporting industry cautions that it has no control over what businesses do when they see a fraud alert).

But Harrison's biggest problem wasn't with the credit bureaus — the key was identifying the bad checks and bogus checking accounts. This is how it works with a fake account: banks return bad checks to merchants, and every merchant who received a bum check wants to get paid (of course). There are hundreds of check management companies that handle processing for merchants, and you often cannot access the information they have unless you know the driver's license number used to cash the check or the bank account number. And since Harrison didn't cash the check or open the account, he knew neither. He didn't even know what bank account they were written on. He only knew the names of the businesses that wanted their money.

Harrison's imposter wrote checks in seven states, and merchants in all seven came after Harrison for 110 bad checks and counting. Merchants eventually hire debt collectors or attorneys to seek payment. Harrison says debt collectors will listen to his saga, express sympathy and then ask if he can make a partial payment. "Debt collectors," he says, "don't care about (resolving issues of) identity theft."

And then, there is the Internal Revenue Service. Late in 2003, Harrison received a letter from the IRS saying he owed $1,900 in taxes on unreported income from 2001. It seems that when a credit card company agreed to erase a $6,400 balance in Harrison's name, the card issuer reported the forgiveness of debt to the IRS, which considers it income.

Harrison has worked seven days a week to clear his name, a stressful situation that cost him his job and his health. He had no choice but to hire an attorney.

Even though victims are usually not saddled with paying their impostors' bills, they are often left with a bad credit report and must spend months and even years regaining their financial health. In the meantime, they have difficulty getting credit, obtaining loans, renting apartments and even getting hired for jobs. Victims of identity theft find little help from legal authorities as they attempt to untangle the web of deception that has allowed another person to impersonate them.

After all the talk about the Information Age being upon us, we might be startled that, actually, it has arrived. Information about us is gathered constantly at grocery stores, banks, credit bureaus and the Internet. Used appropriately, this information makes our lives easier, helps foster the greatest economy in the world and helps reduce a variety of risks — physical and financial.

The downside is, if that information is not protected, it can cost you frustration, time and money.

Unfortunately, stealing your information has become a real business.

Thieves have been known to sell a variety of information for the bargain price of $25.[3] Occasionally, some of them land credit reports and resell these for use in identity theft schemes (In November 2002, federal prosecutors arrested three men who had stolen nearly 30,000 credit reports for just this purpose).

The hackers are not always your stereotypical, pesky, bored, teenaged boys; some are older and very busy. Hackers recently stripped 10 million Visa, MasterCard and American Express numbers from a company that processes transactions for merchants.[4]

Thieves also rattle through mailboxes, looking for the increasingly common unsolicited credit offerings.

When you have a problem, the key lesson is: be persistent in dealing with it. Michael Berry's case shows that, sometimes, the initial contact with the credit bureaus isn't enough to solve the problem. Two bureaus cleaned up his records. One didn't. Berry warns, "If you don't get all three records cleaned up, your credit remains bad."

John Harrison had similar problems.

Harrison says that, out of the 60 fraudulent accounts he has faced, only about a third

Did You Know?

- Even though victims are usually not saddled with paying their impostors' bills, they are often left with a bad credit report and must spend months and even years regaining their financial health.

- Hackers recently stripped 10 million Visa, MasterCard and American Express numbers from a company that processes transactions for merchants.

- Visa USA teamed up in 2003 with a national consumer group to assist identity theft victims. The credit card company and Call for Action have created an identity theft hotline (1-866-ID-HOTLINE) that will provide free and confidential counseling.

of the companies responded to his initial calls and letters. The rest didn't do anything. In some cases, he says, one part of a company would say the problem was being cleared up while another was turning over his account to a collection agency.

Credit bureaus had a spotty history of responding to complaints about identity theft and mistakes. In 1996, Congress amended the Fair Credit Reporting Act to force credit bureaus to be more responsive to people.

"The system works very well but, yes, there are going to be exceptions," says the Chief Privacy Officer of Equifax, John Ford.

He points out even complaints must be checked out to make sure the person complaining is actually the holder of the account and not an ID thief. That takes time.

Credit information is a big business. The bureaus sold about 1.2 billion credit reports in the United States last year, primarily for the legitimate granting of credit. John Harrison tried to use this knowledge to his advantage, calling places that had requested his credit report and asking them to close any accounts opened in his name.

"I thought you could overcome anything with good communication and hard work," Harrison says ruefully, "It was for nothing. They (the merchants who granted credit) would say they didn't have anything and then months later it would show up on a credit report."

Help Is On the Way

The Financial Services Roundtable, which represents 100 institutions handling about 70 percent of the nation's financial transactions, is creating an Identity Theft Assistance Center, scheduled to be operational in 2004. Wells Fargo will pilot the new system beginning in the late Spring. This program will allow people who believe they are victims of identity theft to make one phone call to their local bank, which would then contact the assistance center. The center would obtain an affidavit from the victim to send to law enforcement, credit card companies, financial institutions and credit bureaus. And, financial institutions that receive applications for credit cards or loans could run the requester's name through the center's database to ensure that the person was not the same as an individual who had reported an identity theft.

Visa USA teamed up in 2003 with a national consumer group to assist identity theft victims. The credit card company and Call for Action have created an identity theft hotline **(1-866-ID-HOTLINE)** that will provide free and confidential counseling. Visa also offers identity theft coverage for members **(www.visa.com)**. Many insurers have clued in on this growing market; one of the largest, GEICO **(www.geico.com)**, now offers identity theft coverage.

The USA PATRIOT Act, passed in the aftermath of the September 11 attacks in New York and Washington, D.C., requires banks, mutual funds and insurance agencies to confirm the identification of anyone opening an account. The intention is to help the federal government identify terrorists (many groups connected to Al-Qaeda had accounts in the U.S.) and money launders, and banks must monitor accounts for "suspicious activity."

These precautions, which were urged by the U.S. Treasury, may thwart some identity thieves.

There is also a new version of, the Fair Credit Reporting Act (FCRA), which goes into effect in 2005. It grants consumers new rights and allows everyone a free, annual copy of their credit reports, among other things. You can learn more about, and get a copy, of the FCRA from the Federal Trade Commission at **www.ftc.gov**.

Identity theft currently is rarely pursued by law enforcement agencies because of the time involved and the (relatively) small amount of money lost. The Federal Bureau of Investigation says the average cost of investigating a case is $20,000 per year and can take years to solve.

"Law enforcement has still never, ever investigated the identity fraud part of my case, even after all the publicity," Michael Berry says.

And this, John Harrison agrees, can be maddening.

"When people don't do their jobs, and you lose control, that will drive you nuts," Harrison says. "Five months go by, eight months go by, and you start dealing with problems a second time... places that said they were going to do something and didn't. Everyday, you get home and there are two letters from debt collectors... a phone message from an attorney. That happens over and over and over, for months and months."

Michael Berry, literally, drove around scared for a while. Investigators hot on the trail of his imposter — for the murder charge — were looking for a man of a different race, but because they are so used to law enforcement computers spitting out marred reports, Berry was warned that officers might ignore the race detail if they had the right name.

Six months after stealing Berry's identity, Hunter was arrested. Berry is still dealing with a shredded credit rating. And he keeps letters from the Oakland and Orlando police departments stating "Michael D. Berry is not the felon fugitive that is being sought by several agencies" in his wallet, just in case.

Important Tips

As you can now see, identity theft is a serious and complex issue. There are some basic steps you can take to prevent identity theft and there are a growing number of resources to help if you are the victim. But, the first step to addressing the risks of ID theft begin with you taking personal responsibility for deciding if and how you are going to use the available tools.

If You Want to Protect Your Identity

> The key: actively monitor your identity.

> Don't give out personal information on the phone, through the mail or over the Internet unless you've initiated the contact or are sure you know whom you're dealing with. You can check the organization's Web site, as many companies post scam alerts when their name is used improperly, or you can call customer service using the number listed on your account statement or in the telephone book. Anytime you share personal information, request a copy of the institution's privacy policy and read it.

> Secure personal information in your home, especially if you have roommates, employ outside help or are having service work done in your home.

> When creating passwords and PINs do not use the last four digits of your SSN, mother's maiden name, your birth date, middle name, pet's name, consecutive numbers or anything else that could be easily discovered by thieves. It's best to create passwords that combine letters and numbers.

> Memorize all your passwords. Don't record them on anything in your wallet. Shield your hand when using a bank ATM machine or making long distance phone calls with your phone card. "Shoulder surfers" may be nearby with binoculars or a video camera.

> Deposit outgoing mail in post office collection boxes or at your local post office, rather than in an unsecured mailbox. Promptly remove mail from your mailbox. If you're planning to be away from home and can't pick up your mail, call the U.S. Postal Service at **1-800-275-8777** to request a vacation hold. The Postal Service will hold your mail at your local post office until you can pick it up or are home to receive it.

> Tear or shred your charge receipts, copies of credit applications, insurance forms, physician statements, checks and bank statements, expired charge cards that you're discarding, and credit offers you get in the mail.

> Don't carry your Social Security card; leave it in a secure place. Give your SSN only when absolutely necessary. Ask to use other types of identifiers when possible. If your state uses your SSN as your driver's license number, ask to substitute another number.

> To opt out of receiving pre-screened credit card offers, call: **1-888-5-OPTOUT (1-888-567-8688)**. The three major credit bureaus use the same toll-free number to let consumers choose to not receive pre-screened credit offers. Understand, though, that opting out may mean delays in getting any additional credit in the future while your credit worthiness is checked.

> You can also have your name and address removed from the phone book and reverse directories.

> When ordering new checks, pick them up at the bank. Don't have them mailed to your home. If you have a post office box, use that address on your checks, rather than your home address so thieves will not know where you live.

> Never use public computers (for instance, in a library or cyber-cafe) to pay bills or divulge other personal information. Expect that any information placed on that computer remains there for thieves.

> Check your credit report at least once a year. The most sweeping change in credit laws in years will soon allow consumers to have one free copy of their credit report each year from each credit-reporting agency. Check with the major credit bureaus to learn when and how you can get your free annual report.

> The major credit bureaus and other financial companies offer monitoring services that alert you to changes to your credit status and credit report. Check with the credit bureaus to see if their monitoring products are for you:

Equifax sells *Equifax Credit Watch*
Experian sells *Credit Manager*
Transunion sells *Transunion Monitoring Service*

The three major credit bureaus are:

Equifax — www.equifax.com
To order your report, call: **1-800-685-1111**
or write: P.O. Box 740241, Atlanta, GA 30374-0241
To report fraud, call: **1-800-525-6285**
and write: P.O. Box 740241, Atlanta, GA 30374-0241

Experian — www.experian.com
To order your report, call: **1-888-EXPERIAN (397-3742)**
or write: P.O. Box 2104, Allen, TX 75013
To report fraud, call: **1-888-EXPERIAN (397-3742)**
and write: P.O. Box 9532, Allen, TX 75013

TransUnion — www.transunion.com
To order your report, call: **1-800-916-8800**
or write: P.O. Box 1000, Chester, PA 19022
To report fraud, call: **1-800-680-7289**
and write: Fraud Victim Assistance Division,
P.O. Box 6790, Fullerton, CA 92834-6790

> Contact the fraud department of any one of the three major credit bureaus to place a fraud alert on your credit file at all three bureaus. This requests creditors to contact you before opening any new accounts or making changes to your existing accounts. You do *not* have to be an identity theft victim to place a "fraud alert" on your three credit reports. It is just an extra layer of protection to help cut down on the possibility of

identity theft. Remember, though, placing a fraud alert on your file will delay any application for credit until you can be contacted by a credit bureau verifying you are seeking new credit.

If Your Identity Is Stolen

> Pay attention to your billing cycles. Follow up with creditors if your bills don't arrive on time. A missing credit card bill could mean an identity thief has taken over your account and changed your billing address to cover his tracks.

> Keep a copy of your credit card, bank account and investment account numbers, as well as expiration dates and telephone numbers of the customer service and fraud departments in a secure place so you can quickly contact these companies in case your credit cards have been stolen or accounts are being used fraudulently. Don't keep them in your wallet. Close the accounts that you know or believe have been tampered with.

> Notify the three major credit bureaus and request that a fraud alert be placed on your file. **Please note:** Fraud alerts and victim statements are voluntary services provided by the credit bureaus. Creditors do not have to consider them when granting credit. That's why it's vital to continue checking your reports periodically. In addition, fraud alerts and victim statements expire; you need to renew them periodically. Ask each bureau about its policy.

> Periodically check public records to see if anyone has been convicted of committing a crime using your identity. ChoicePoint offers a criminal record self-check at **www.choicetrust.com**.

> Request major check verification companies notify retailers who use their databases not to accept your stolen checks. You can also find out if the identity thief has been passing bad checks in your name. The major check verification companies are:

Certegy, Inc.
1-800-437-5120

SCAN
1-800-262-7771

TeleCheck
1-800-366-2425

ChexSystems
1-800-428-9623

> Contact your local and state authorities to find out if they pursue identity theft cases. Even if your police department will not pursue the case, file a police report. Get a copy of the report to submit to your creditors and others that may require proof of the crime.

> Use the ID Theft Affidavit, available through the Federal Trade Commission, when disputing new, unauthorized accounts. You can find the form at **www.ftc.gov** or request one at **1-202-326-2222**. You can also use the Broderbund Identity Theft Software **(www.broderbund.com)**. It provides all the forms needed to address identity theft.

> Organize your case. This will really improve your chances of resolution. Follow up in writing with all contacts you've made on the phone or in person. Use certified mail, return receipt requested. Keep copies of all correspondence or forms you send. Write down the name of anyone you talk to, what he or she told you and the date the conversation occurred. Keep the originals of supporting documentation, like police reports, and letters to and from creditors; send copies only. Set up a filing system for easy access to your paperwork. Keep old files even if you believe your case is closed. One of the most difficult and annoying aspects of identity theft is that errors can reappear on your credit reports or your information can be re-circulated. Should this happen, you'll be glad you kept your files.

> Some other helpful Web sites if you are a victim of identity theft include:

> **www.usdoj.gov/criminal/fraud/idtheft.html**

> **www.consumer.gov/idtheft/**

> **www.privacyrights.org/itrc-quiz1.htm**

Let's Talk

These questions will help you, your family and others to begin a discussion about issues covered in this chapter.

1. To what kind of identity theft are we most vulnerable?
2. How are we protecting ourselves from identity theft?
3. Should we do more? What should we do?
4. Do we know what to do if our identities are stolen?

CHAPTER 2: **Cyber Safety**

Your Computer's Secret Social Life

All Lorraine Sullivan wanted to do was find some new music and listen to it. Like 60 million other people around the world, she didn't think much about downloading a few songs onto her computer.

"I never thought at the time about the ethics of it. I was doing the same thing you do when you record a song off the radio."

Sullivan was a student at Hunter College in New York. She downloaded software, which made her computer part of a peer-to-peer (P2P) network. That meant anyone using her computer could upload or download songs into the Kazaa system. Sullivan maintains that's exactly what happened — other students used her computer to access free music.

She says she didn't know her entire file of songs was then open to sharing through the P2P network.

But the music industry, through the Recording Industry Association of America (RIAA), discovered it and made Sullivan one of the unlucky 261 people slapped with a lawsuit.

It turns out they knew exactly what was on her computer.

It's a brave new world, all right; a world where what's on your computer may become known to others. Because Internet usage can be tracked and monitored, personal preferences can become public and communication can be intercepted.

New terms like "spyware," "snoopware," and "cookies" are dropped in conversation — but what the heck *are* these things? And who is doing what to whom? It is a world brought closer through technology, but what can we do to protect ourselves from these computer invaders?

Understanding the risks is the first step.

Computer Security Blanket

The first thing you do after flipping on your computer is type in your password. This is your shot at creativity — you get to name the key to your computer's soul! — but, alas, many people fail miserably. Your kid's name, your maiden name, your pet's name, and — believe it or not — one of the most common passwords is "password." The lackadaisical attitude most of us take to the naming of our password is understandable; after all, how many hackers out there are salivating to break into your files to snatch your family recipe for barbeque sauce?

It is a trusting approach, but not practical anymore. Passwords are the first line of defense to protecting your computer system and just about everything requires them. You might be juggling ten different passwords, which is difficult to keep straight. In fact, many people solve this problem by writing down their passwords and keeping them in a desk drawer or even stuck on the computer screen itself. Once a password is chosen, chances are you will keep it for a long time. All of this is an absolute dream to a hacker.

Those most at risk keep their computers online all the time via a broadband or DSL line. That gives hackers time to play around.

A hacker who is committed to entering your system will first run a program that can contain whole dictionaries from several different languages and words from movies and novels in an attempt to guess the correct password.

Keep in mind that — depending on how you use your personal computer — a thief may not need to set foot in your house to rob you. Social Security numbers, financial records, tax returns, birth dates and bank account numbers may be stored in your computer — a goldmine to an identity thief.

Don't give them the chance to steal your good name.

Important Tips

> Install a firewall on your home computer to protect your personal identification and financial data stored on your hard drive from hackers. This is especially important if you connect to the Internet by DSL or cable modem because these services are always connected.

> Create a password that combines six to eight numbers and letters, upper and lower case, in a random way. Password protect files that contain sensitive personal data, such as financial account information.

> Change your password an average of every 60 days, which is how long it would take an attacker on a very fast computer to figure it out, according to the Department of Homeland Security.

> Don't use an automatic login feature. It may be convenient (it's hard to remember more than a handful of passwords), but anyone who has access to your computer can use it.

> For the very security-conscious, there are credit card-sized scanners that replace your password with a fingerprint. You can even buy a fingerprint reader for your laptop computer. Several major electronics companies like Sony, Compaq and Targus offer these biometric login devices.

Did You Know?

- Passwords are the first line of defense to protecting your computer system and just about everything requires them.

- Those most at risk keep their computers online all the time via a broadband or DSL line. That gives hackers time to play around.

> Use the most up-to-date secure browsers — software that encrypts or scrambles information you send over the Internet — to guard the security of your online transactions. When submitting information, look for the "lock" icon on the browser's status bar to be sure your information is secure during transmission.

> No matter how you log in, always log off when finished.

> When it's time to replace your computer, there is still one last security task to complete. Before disposing of the computer, remove data by using a strong "wipe" utility program. Do not rely on the "delete" function to remove files containing sensitive information. For more information, see Clearing Information From Your Computer's Hard Drive (**www.hq.nasa.gov/office/oig/hq/harddrive.pdf**) from the National Aeronautics and Space Administration (NASA).

Spam

The best password protection can't prevent folks from obtaining your e-mail address if you use it widely.

And once your e-mail address is known, expect an invasion of spam.

Spam is a canned good many enjoyed pan-frying on Saturday afternoon for lunch. It is also the bombardment of junk mail that can outright ruin a good e-mail address.

There are people who make money doing this. One of them, the prolific Richard Colbert, prefers the term "bulk e-mailing" to "spamming."[1] They get your e-mail address a variety of ways, like a software program called a spider (it crawls through Web pages, searching for the telltale @ symbol) and those handy member directories you might have filled out when you signed up for an Internet service.

Sometimes, spammers manage to obtain your e-mail address through less-than-ethical means. In October 2003, an online travel agency notified law enforcement officials that a security breach allowed spammers to get the e-mail addresses of a small number of customers.[2]

Spam is hard to stop. Despite the best efforts of the anti-Spam forces, spammers always seem to figure out a way around the filters. It's a constant game of cat and mouse. Congress has passed, and President Bush has signed into law, new measures aimed at cutting spam. But it's doubtful the law will end the annoyance because enforcement is difficult and the law doesn't apply to companies outside the United States. That means spammers may be able to get around the law by setting up shop anywhere in the world there's a computer and telephone service.

Important Tips

> The best way to treat spam of the e-mail variety is to throw it in the (computer) trash can without opening it. If you open it to "unsubscribe," the spammer who sent it to you now knows the address is "live" and there is a person at the other end. That's gold to a spammer.

> Carefully read the fine print when you purchase a product or service online. Often times, there are check boxes where you can opt-out of receiving information you didn't request. The same is true when you buy something in the "real" world, where increasingly you are asked to supply an e-mail address.

> It may not be captivating reading, but do read the privacy policy of online and offline companies you do business with. Some companies will sell your e-mail address. If they do, they will disclose that in their privacy policy. If you don't want your e-mail address sold, don't provide the information or consider doing business elsewhere.

Did You Know?

- Cookies are pieces of information generated from Web sites and stored in the user's computer, ready for future access.

- Cookies cannot harm your computer or pass on private information like an e-mail address unless the user volunteers that information.

- You may not fully realize it, but your computer is likely filled with these morsels.

> Treat your e-mail address as you would your physical address or unlisted telephone number — don't give it to anyone you don't want to use it. Many Internet service providers allow you to have multiple e-mail addresses. Set up one just for the purpose of giving out to online and offline merchants.

> Type your e-mail address on the Web as "Jack at hotmail.com" instead of using the @ symbol. This will help prevent spiders from capturing e-mail addresses from your computer.

> Check with your Internet Service Provider to see if they offer a Spam blocker.

> Look for security companies like McAfee (**www.mcafee.com**), Symantec (**www.symantec.com**), ZoneAlarm (**www.zonealarm.com**) and Global Security Solutions (sold by a variety of retailers) and Internet Service Providers offering anti-virus programs and personal firewalls. Update your virus protection software often. These programs can prevent a virus or worm from causing your computer to send out files or other stored information.

Cookies

Cookies are pieces of information generated from Web sites and stored in the user's computer, ready for future access. The first batch of cookies was cooked up as a mechanism to make it easier for users to access their favorite sites by storing passwords. Now, these files contain information on what sites you visit, how long you visited the site, if you made any purchases, where else you went, your name, even your credit card number. When you visit the most popular Web sites or click on any ad, a cookie is generated and set on your computer. Fortunately, they are generally benign.

The questions about cookies begin when the string of information grows longer. If you fill out a form, for example, that asks you to give yourself an online name, your real name, your income, maybe even your address — all of this can be stored in your cookie.

In a recent government report, officials deemed cookie technology generally okay, although the report also pointed out some cookies are persistent and track people's browsing habits for a long time.[3]

The report stressed that there is a sense of paranoia involved with cookies, but that cookies cannot harm your computer or pass on private information like an e-mail address unless the user volunteers that information.

The two-stage process goes like this: first, the cookie is stored in your computer. For instance, a customized Web search engine like My Yahoo! allows you to select categories of interest from the Web page. The Web page server then creates a specific cookie — a string of text containing your preferences — and transmits this cookie to your computer. Your Web browser, if it accepts cookies, receives the cookie and stores it in a special file called a cookie list.

Personal information (your category preferences) is formatted by the Web server, transmitted and saved by your computer.

Then the information contained in the cookie is automatically transferred from your computer to a Web server so that whenever you direct your Web browser to display a certain Web page from the server, the browser will transmit the information you want quickly.

Or your bank may ask you to provide certain information so that when you return to its Web site, future transactions take less time thanks to the information stored in the cookie.

You may not fully realize it, but your computer is likely filled with these morsels. That means it's important to periodically look at your cookies to make sure you aren't storing any from sites you no longer visit.

- *Spyware* is a common term for files that are installed on your system that allow other people to monitor your Internet activity.

- Sometimes *spyware* is placed on a company computer to track employee usage of a corporate computer, a perfectly legal business practice.

- *Snoopware* is different from spyware in that it can be installed remotely.

- *Adware* is another secretly downloaded file. It's designed to create pop up advertisements on your computer screen whether you want them or not.

Important Tips

> If you do not want cookies on your computer, if asked, simply decline to accept them.

> Most of the time, you aren't asked if you want to accept cookies. To stop cookies, you must use a firewall or adjust the security settings of your Web browser so it does not download cookies. If you don't know where to find the security settings on your computer, look under the "help" tab or check the manual that came with your computer. Remember, if you set your computer to reject all cookies, you may not be able to use certain Web sites or you will be forced to re-enter your information each time you visit a site.

> If you want to erase your cookie files or folders, this can be done manually simply by locating and deleting the cookie files on your hard drive. Be sure to close your browser before you begin.

Spyware, Snoopware and Adware

If you think cookies or spam are fattening (and annoying), spyware, snoopware and adware just might cause indigestion.

Spyware is a common term for files that are installed on your system that allow other people to monitor your Internet activity. Sometimes it is placed on a company computer to track employee usage of a corporate computer, a perfectly legal business practice.

It can also be used to block your e-mail from particular senders, stop you from printing documents deemed too sensitive, and record instant-messaging conversations among workers. Responsible organizations inform employees they are using spyware.

Snoopware is different from spyware in that it can be installed remotely. For instance, one snoopware company claimed to let owners "spy on anyone by sending them an e-mail greeting card." There remain questions whether this violates federal wiretapping laws.[4]

These products are on the market, claim manufacturers, for use by parents who want to make sure their children are protected online and by companies who want to monitor employees. Buyers typically must acknowledge in a disclaimer that they promise to use the technology legally. However, manufacturers do admit that snoopware can be used illegally. "A car can run somebody over. That doesn't mean you design a car to run over somebody," one manufacturer told CBS News.[5]

Adware is another secretly downloaded file. It's designed to create pop up advertisements on your computer screen whether you want them or not.

Like spyware, it can be brought home through pop-ups, Web pages, spam, instant messages or vulnerable browser settings. As the name implies, you won't know it's there until it begins to do its work of generating unwanted advertisement and even redirecting your home page.

The spyware and adware you download are all legal, at least for now. A federal judge in Virginia ruled consumers consent to taking pop-up ads and even spyware when they choose to download the software.

All of these "ware" products bring with them an admonishment to be "aware." There are products available to help block the unwanted varieties of spyware, snoopware and adware. It's not uncommon for a parent of teenagers who use instant messaging products or an online power shopper to install a filter that identifies nearly a thousand unwanted and undetected objects the first time a scan is run.

Important Tips

> At work, ask about your company's policy on monitoring employee use of company computers. Remember, it's a common practice and legal, but it's also considered to be good policy to disclose the monitoring practices.

> Look for anti-spyware, snoopware and adware programs such as the free programs Spybot Search & Destroy (**www.spybot.com**) and LanSoft Ad-Aware (free downloads from **www.cnet.com**), also, InterMute (**www.intermute.com**). Be sure to set up routine scans that check for product updates and scan your files for new, unwanted wares.

> Be careful when you download files, especially those sent to you by strangers. The same is true of clicking on hyperlinks from businesses or people you don't know. Opening a file could expose your system to more spyware, snoopware, adware, a computer virus or a program that could hijack your computer.

> Think twice before opening a pop-up ad, especially if it's from a company you don't know. Snoopware, and adware are often attached to pop-ups and occasionally from banner ads. The worst of these will redirect your home page.

Caught in the Act

Even after you gain an understanding about the nuts and bolts of computer safety, there remain questions over the law as it pertains to computer usage.

For instance, you may have greater legal protection at home than in the workplace or when using computers in public areas.

"At home, there is the issue of expectations of privacy," says John Mayoue, a prominent family law attorney from Atlanta.

But think of e-mail that you receive at a home computer as you do regular U.S. postal mail: it is illegal to open someone else's mail (unless you give them your password). If you have password protection and your e-mail is opened or read through spyware by someone other than you, that person has broken the law.

One area of e-mail that is shaky is in the realm of marital relations. Suspicious husbands and wives who might have once turned to a private detective to find out if their spouses were cheating are now using technology. The Internet is a popular place for trysts, and evidence can be gathered through tracking e-mails and chat room activity, and this in turn has created a whole new market for electronic spying.

Web sites like **www.Chatcheaters.com** and **www.InfidelityCheck.org** offer an array of surveillance products, including a kind of spyware that can monitor each keystroke in real time.

Chatcheaters was established by a man whose wife of 23 years abruptly left him and their two teenage daughters to live with a New Zealand man she had met online. Chatcheaters averages 400 visitors a day (mostly women), who can purchase $100 computer spying programs, as well as other high-tech surveillance measures (such as $450 vehicle trackers).

Mayoue, who has handled many high-profile divorce cases, says that a suspicious husband or wife may have no legal grounds for breaking pass-word-protected areas of a spouse's personal computer. But, that e-mail that was easily retrieved on the family computer (possibly through spyware or snoopware placed there by your spouse), that is a little less clear.

And, remember, you have no right to remove spyware legally placed on your work computer if you've been notified.

"What you should keep in mind," Mayoue, the Atlanta lawyer says, "is that if you're making communications over a business computer, you do so at your own risk. Whereas telephone calls made in the workplace cannot be tapped, as far as computers go, the watchword is never use the company computer for something you don't want anyone to see."

That includes e-mails.

Mayoue believes a strict interpretation of the law could potentially allow employers to be prosecuted for reading employee e-mail, but this is one area where he believes the law is in a perennial state of catch-up. There is plenty of legislation dealing with telephones and wiretapping, but not for computers, even though far more personal information is readily available there.

Public Computers

Public access computers aren't just for libraries anymore. You can find free terminals in coffee houses, car washes, airports, shop-

In this new world of universal access you should assume that anything you write on a computer in a public area can be retrieved by someone, both for proper and improper reasons.

ping malls and just about anywhere else people gather. In this new world of universal access you should assume that anything you write on a computer in a public area can be retrieved by someone, both for proper and improper reasons.

A good rule to follow is that if you use a computer that is not your own, ask yourself, "Do I want anyone to see what I'm doing?" And the criminal minds out there have been putting this high tech "look over the shoulder" to use. A New York man recently pleaded guilty to putting monitoring software on computers at a photocopy store so he could steal credit card account numbers. A college student in Boston is charged with using a keystroke-logging program to steal an investment account password to facilitate a stock scam.[6]

On public computers, even if you clear the temporary files, don't assume you've solved the problem. Those files can still be recovered by someone intent on finding them.

Important Tips

> Never use computers in public spaces for banking, e-mailing or any other functions you wish to keep private and personal.

> If you log on to a favorite site using a public computer, always remember to log off. Otherwise, the next user will be able to access the sites you visited using your password.

Music Downloading

When is the information on my computer not mine? That's the issue at the heart of the argument over music downloading.

The music industry has declared war against the pirates who, it says, are stealing intellectual property. And despite questions from senators like Norm Coleman of Minnesota (who wonders if lawsuits alone can stop the download-ing), the Recording Industry Association of America (RIAA) told a Senate committee that it was not about to back off of its tough stance. Under the Digital Millennium Copyright Act, copyright holders can retrieve information about people who download music. The fines for illegally downloading music through peer-to-peer (P2P) file-sharing networks range from a few thousand dollars to $150,000 per song.[7]

Lorraine Sullivan says, "I was shocked and it was scary to think that complete strangers could look into my computer and see everything."

"I can see if my song is on there and 10,000 people download it, that's wrong. But the way the whole thing was handled was wrong. It's about educating people. Most people didn't know about the ethical problem."

Sullivan ended up settling the suit rather than fighting the Big Five record companies and the RIAA for $2,500.

Senator Coleman (who was a roadie for ten years for Jethro Tull and Savoy Brown) has publicly stated that the law is not being used properly, and that the fines are not appropriate. "There is nothing in current law that restricts the scope of the RIAA's use of subpoenas to ferret out unlawful downloaders," he said during his own recent committee hearing.

The record industry uses software to scan the download sites, according to Wendy Seltzer, the attorney for the Electronic Freedom Foundation. "People are being targeted as a function of what they are doing on peer-to-peer networks," she says. "The simplest way to avoid being sued is to avoid offering files for upload. That doesn't mean you have to stop using the peer networks, only that you stop offering files for upload."

Alan Morris, who runs Sharman Networks Ltd., the parent company of Kazaa, maintains that Kazaa has installed filters and other tools to limit illegal downloads, and that his clients should not be treated like criminals. "The issue here doesn't seem to be about copyright," he testified before the Senate. "It seems to be about control over distribution."

Senator Sam Brownback (R-KS) maintains that this is an issue of privacy, not piracy. He warns that without some changes to the law, "Salespersons, ex-spouses, absolute strangers — anyone can pose as a copyright owner and obtain your name, address and telephone number." He wrote in the Wall Street Journal: "Your safety is threatened...imagine what pedophiles and stalkers could do with this power to track down their targets."[8]

Brownback and those who agree with him won a major court battle late in 2003 when a federal appeals court ruled in favor of Internet Service Provider Verizon and against the RIAA.

The three-judge panel ruled that the simple assertion of a copyright infringement is not enough to force the Internet Service Provider to turn over the identities of customers who use P2P networks to share music. If the ruling holds, the RIAA would have to use the more time consuming method of filing an actual lawsuit against a suspected copyright infringer.

This is ultimately a battle where the courts will continue to weigh the sometimes competing interests of copyright holders, service providers and individuals.

Important Tips

> Make sure you limit use of your personal computer to those you are sure you can trust. If someone using your computer breaks a law or regulation, the violation may be traced back to your computer.

> Make sure that your shared files contain only files that are in the public domain, that you have permission to share, or that are available under pro-sharing licenses such as the Creative Common license or other open media licenses.

> Remove all potentially misleading file names that might be confused with the same of an RIAA artist or song (like "Justin Timberlake" or "Pink").

> Disable the "sharing" or "uploading" features on your P2P application that allow other users on the network to get copies of files from your computer or scan any of your music directories.

I See You, You See Me

There is a related issue: information ABOUT you, but not taken from a computer you use. Instead, this is information flowing through the Internet that is public information, for the most part. Still, it is surprising for many people to see just how much information is available.

For instance, you can type a phone number into a Google search and not only does the name of the person with that number come up, but also their address, courtesy of MapQuest (having an unlisted phone number prevents this or you can click on the phone icon and fill out a form). All of this has been in the White Pages for decades. But now, it can be found worldwide instantly.

Ever been in the newspaper? It's there on the Internet. Ever owned a piece of property, owned a business or had a professional license. It's generally all there in some form on the Web.

The great Google, the most popular search engine, has even spawned its own verb. New York Times columnist Maureen Dowd admitted, in print, to "googling" prospective dates. Countless others use it before a business meeting or an interview, or even to organize far-flung class reunions. It all makes finding information about people much easier, but also scares some people.

It is important to know what information is available about you in the vast reaches of cyberspace. Much of the data comes from public sources where you willingly and knowingly provided the information. Good privacy policies are based on transparency, and are designed to ensure you know how your information is going to be used. Still, a good policy doesn't relieve you of your duty to ask about the ways your personal information is going to be used so you can make an informed decision.

 Let's Talk

These questions will help you, your family and others to begin a discussion about issues covered in this chapter.

1. What kind of computer security is right for us? Do we need or have a firewall, virus protection, spam blocker and spyware, snoopware and adware detection?

2. Do we know who is using our computer and for what reason? Are we only uploading and downloading items that we know are legally available and free from unwanted "spiders?"

3. Do we know how to change the security settings on our computer? Are they the right settings for the level of risk we face?

4. Do we use public computers for private activities like checking e-mail, paying bills and visiting password-protected sites?

5. Do we read online and offline privacy policies so we know what information is being collected about us, how it will be used and if it will be sold or shared? Will we have an opportunity to say "no?"

CHAPTER 3: **Buyer Beware**

Attention Online Shoppers!

Here is a nice story about how a young elementary school teacher, living in a small town, never really having had a boyfriend, gave up on love after trying the usual routes of bars, friends and fate (because love could just *happen*, couldn't it?)

At 33, Ann Rolfe (not her real name) decided that she would never, ever find anybody.

And then, she went relationship shopping.

"I decided I needed to be a little proactive," Rolfe says, "So I went on Match.com."

She posted her own profile about a woman who loves country music and long walks. She also perused the profiles of men.

Rolfe wasn't looking for tall, dark, handsome and loaded. She just wanted "kind." She suffered through a few less-than-kind dinner dates, and nearly gave up, before she met Frank Aubrey (also not his real name) for Thai food.

He was tall, sandy-haired and handsome. *And* kind.

Fourteen months later, they are engaged. They will be married in August 2004.

"I can't wait," Rolfe says. "I get to spend the rest of my life with him."

Looking for Love

That is the light, happy side of Internet relationships. Technology has improved communication, and in an age when it does sometimes seem impossible to meet Mr. or Miss Right, Web sites like Match.com, Matchmaker, JDate.com, eCRUSH, eHarmony and Lavalife have taken the place of the proverbial village matchmaker. It can be a wonderful thing, when it happens right.

And then, there is the darker side, prowled by shadowy con-men (and women), liars, cheats, scam artists, criminals and downright disturbed individuals. Not just in the venue of dating, either. The advent of online shopping, with its ease and convenience, has its own scams, fake sites and all-around fraud. How can anyone expect to wade through technology and the darker side of humanity?

Nearly 6 million people are hitting the Internet to find their match. The personal sites like Lavalife are dominated by men; women prefer more romance-related sites, such as those that also sell flowers or provide greetings. But no matter where they go, they *are* going. Romance site visits rose nearly 50 percent in the last year, which is more than double the rate of increase of general Web use.

The first step is picking a service. There are many; some like JDate.com and Catholicsinglesonline.com, that focus on religion; others, like GoodGenes.com (which takes only Ivy League graduates), cater to specific requirements.

It's up to you to decide how much information to share online.

Usually, sites will ask for personal information (which may or may not be kept confidential) and you can browse subscriber profiles or post one of your own. Then, either you receive e-mail from interested parties or you contact them.

Most people who pursue Internet dating are optimistic that they could meet not just a date online, but also perhaps their soul mates. A survey conducted by Match.com showed that most online singles are seeking a relationship that leads to long-term commitment or marriage, and that more than half of them are positive that they will find true love within the next year.

"It worked for me!" Rolfe says cheerfully.

And then, there is what happened to Lisa Hupman.

"I had met so many guys from newspaper personal ads, I figured I could spot a jerk a mile away," Hupman says ruefully. "Nuh-uh! The net's different. You *think* you can tell if someone is legit or not because you watch their thought processes as they type. You *perceive* emotions that aren't there and you miss the clues that are staring you in the face."

Hupman met "a cute little guy" who was a musician. After a month of e-mailing and chatting, the musician invited her to his house, across the country, with her daughter for the holidays. From the start, the visit went badly.

The cute little guy, who had portrayed himself as a stable, financially secure civil servant, was suddenly jobless. The utilities, including the electricity, were about to be shut off. And then, while tooling around town with the new man in her life, Hupman spied the car of her dreams. Her guy promised to drive it out to her in California; after all, he was coming out in a few weeks, anyway, for an interview.

Hupman got home and called the car dealer. He was a little surprised to hear from her because, he explained, she had already stopped by with her boyfriend to pick up the car.

"Seems I am a petite blonde who sounds a lot like his ex-girlfriend," Hupman says. "They faxed me a copy of the contract and his name was on it. And then, the guy tells me he's not coming to California but he can manage the car payments. So I called the police, and they were on it! That is, at least, until they called the guy and he told them we met on the Internet. They shut me out like I had the plague."

Ultimately, the police did act on a forgery charge — Hupman's musician had forged a check made out to her — and Hupman got HER car back.

"I figured it was an isolated incident," she says, "but I did start to look for familiar phrases. I suddenly discovered a whole bunch of men, all over the country, went to the same school! I knew which phrases to be wary of, which guys to run from and which guys to avoid completely."

But there is a happy ending to this story too.

Hupman didn't give up. She later met the man she would marry on the Internet and now has a four-year-old son. And she started her own Web site, **www.wildangel.com**, to help people survive the slings and arrows of Internet dating.

"Love on the Internet is not possible," she says. "That's not to say you won't meet the person who will become your lover, but don't let it languish or linger online. Meet quickly. The more time you spend online, the higher the expectations in real life. Invariably, the conversations online will turn to sex, and when that happens, the expectation for the first meeting is almost unbearably high. And then, you have to be very secure. If you buy into the Internet hype, play online games, have online friends, then every aspect of your life will exist there as well. Hold it together, never wear your heart on your sleeve."

Understand the people you meet online may not be exactly like their descriptions. In fact, they may not exist at all. Some online daters create completely fictitious alter egos, sometimes as part of an identity fraud scheme like those described in Chapter One, but more often because they are attempting to hide something about themselves.

But the Internet has been an effective way of bringing together like-minded people. You can protect yourself by following a few basic guidelines.

 Important Tips

> Find out if the Web site does anything to determine whether the people participating in their online community are who they say they are AND are what they say they are.

> You can also do a background check on yourself and offer to trade it with one done by a potential companion if the Web site doesn't perform a check.

> Find out if the Web site works to protect the personal information you share with the site.

> Initially, be vague about geographical information — don't give your exact town or neighborhood.

> Think before giving out your phone number. If someone suggests you call them collect, remember that your phone number will appear on

their phone bill. Also, activate the Caller ID blocking feature so that your phone number remains "private."

> Select your handle carefully. "HotMama," for instance can indicate you are seeking a certain kind of attention; you are not likely to meet Mr. or Ms. Right with that. Think about your best qualities and the kind of person you want to attract and choose your handle from there.

> Be careful about bragging. It's easy to think you need to present *all* your good points, but proceed with caution. Too much information sends out an invitation to those who would defraud you.

> Remember your manners. Maintain some decorum when exploring personal and chat sites.

These final observations:

> Pay careful attention to your online companions. Do they sound too good to be true in those e-mails? Are the details a little too vague? Pin them down on the details — if they are evasive, consider that a red flag.

> If you are left with answers that don't make sense (but the person you are e-mailing has a quick explanation), ask yourself more than once: is he/she really believable? For example, "I'd love to meet you soon, but I have some personal matters to take care of first."

> Know what they really look like. Many are the man or woman who "fell" for a cyber pal only to be shocked when they saw that pal for the very first time. A good way to know if it is a current photo is to ask for the person to hold up a copy of that day's newspaper — the date will be impossible to read, but the day's headline won't be hard to miss.

> Anyone who tells you they love you within the first week of knowing you online is most likely not telling the truth. Sure, there might be infatuations or an overwhelming desire to meet, but a rule of thumb is anyone who declares their loving devotion that early is probably a "confidence" man (or woman). That con is to put you at ease immediately, agree with everything you say, and pour out undying emotions. Step back and tell them you are doing so. If it really is love, then it will stand a test of a few weeks.

Looking for a Deal

If shopping for a partner has become increasingly popular in the last couple years, regular online shopping is one of the fastest growing areas of retail.

And no wonder. In 1998, only 25 million homes regularly went online; within two years, this number had doubled, and today two out of three people in the U.S. use the Internet. The telephone took 50 years to reach this level of saturation; television took 30 years.[1]

E-commerce is expected to hit an estimated $6.8 trillion in 2004, so it should not be surprising that fraud on the Internet has risen sharply. In its' most recent report (for 2002), the FBI noted more than 48,000 complaints referred to prosecutors — triple the number of the year before. The total dollar loss of Internet fraud reported in 2002 was $54 million, compared with $17 million the year before. One case alone involved $800,000 in losses: Three hundred people bought computers online and never received their merchandise. Nearly 43 percent of all reported Internet fraud comes from auction fraud, according to the FBI and the National White Collar Crime Center.[2]

> It is important to know the seller's reputation. If you're not familiar with the name and reputation of a company — and especially if a seller has sent you an unsolicited e-mail message, you should do your due diligence.

Still, there is no denying the convenience and ease of shopping on the Internet. James Randall and his wife Lisa Bunting (their names have been changed here) say that from their home in Atlanta, they do nearly all their business online — from banking to paying bills to purchasing clothing, and travel arrangements.

"You don't get instant gratification," Randall says, "You can't buy a CD at a store and listen to it on the way home. It does take away a little bit of the thrill of the hunt." But then again, it takes Randall months to find a rare CD at a store and only a few minutes to find it online.

They haven't had any trouble with returns; they trust their credit card company to cover them in cases of fraud (most credit card companies do). And, they find bargains.

"One of our favorite sites is overstock.com," Bunting says.

There *are* good deals, convenience and many choices on the Internet. And there are ways to be "cyber" smart about it.

One of the most important things to keep in mind while shopping online is making sure the Internet connection is secure. Many Web sites use Secure Sockets Layer (SSL) technology to encrypt the credit card information that you send over the Internet. These sites usually inform you they are using this technology. Or, check if the Web address on the page that asks for your credit card information begins with "https:" instead of "http:"; if so, this technology is in place. A different security technology, which works on different principles, is Secure Electronic Transaction, or SET, technology. SET or SSL technology are designed to make your connection secure.

Another hot topic to watch out for is the scourge of e-mails sweeping the country, pretending to help consumers. One such e-mail, supposedly from the online auction site eBay, asked eBay customers to reenter their personal information — and credit card numbers — as they had recently been lost; as a result, thousands of eBay consumers were defrauded. These e-mails will often direct you to a Web site that *looks* official. The FBI advises if you receive such e-mails, don't give out the information and don't delete the e-mail — yet. File a complaint first with the Internet Fraud Center (**www.ifccfbi.gov**) and *then* delete it.

It is important to know the seller's reputation. If you're not familiar with the name and reputation of a company — and especially if a seller has sent you an unsolicited e-mail message, you should do your due diligence. You can check a company's reputation by contacting the Better Business Bureau or the Office of the State Attorney General in your state or the state where the seller is located, which can be accessed through the National Association of Attorneys General. If you are buying from an individual, for instance, on an auction site like eBay, there are usually "feedback" areas where customers can discuss their experiences with a particular person auctioning off goods.

Sometimes sites are fake. One way to find out if a Web business is legitimate is to

Did You Know?

- In 1998, only 25 million homes regularly went online; within two years, this number had doubled, and today two out of three people in the U.S. use the Internet.

- E-commerce is expected to hit an estimated $6.8 trillion in 2004, so it should not be surprising that fraud on the Internet has risen sharply.

- The total dollar loss of Internet fraud reported in 2002 was $54 million, compared with $17 million the year before.

- Nearly 43 percent of all reported Internet fraud comes from auction fraud.

Did You Know?

look on the site for a street address and phone number. You should be wary if the seller's only contact information is a post office box. You also should check if the seller is out of business by telephoning or sending an e-mail, particularly if the Web site's material appears to be old or out of date.

It's not a bad idea to seek out authorized sellers by calling the manufacturer of the product you're interested in, or visit the manufacturer's Web site to check if the operator of the site has been authorized to sell the manufacturer's product. You may get better warranty service if you buy from an authorized seller.

If you are a bargain hunter like James Randall and Lisa Bunting, then you probably know that some Web sites offer an "electronic agent" to identify the sites that charge the lowest price for a specified product. Be aware that some sellers have taken technological steps to block these "agents" from gathering pricing data. In addition, "agent" sites might not take shipping costs or return/refund policies into account when comparing the prices.

If there is a small crisis of confidence happening, credit card companies are trying to help. Visa, for example, started its *Verified by Visa* password whenever you want to make a purchase on a Web site and is exploring the possibility of using voice recognition to verify online purchases in the future.

Still, scams abound out there on the World Wide Web. eBay now issues warnings about scam e-mails and spoof Web sites in its *Announcements* section about every two or three weeks.

"Because the scam e-mails usually convey a sense of urgency, it's easy to react too quickly. For example, there might be a letter that says your account has been hacked, and you have to hurry and change your password or else your auctions will be ended," David Steiner told Internetnews.com. Steiner's Web site, AuctionBytes, covers the world of online auctions. "There's a constant pool of potential new victims as new sellers sign on to eBay, and I still see a consistently steady stream of scam e-mails."[3]

Steiner has also seen scam deals. One that he tracked on **www.AuctionBytes.com** involved a man who thought he'd come across his dream car on eBay. After the auction ended without meeting its reserve, the man contacted the seller to see if he would be willing to sell it to him. They agreed on a price of $36,000, and the man wired the payment to the seller's bank account using **www.Escrowoncall.net**, a service suggested by the seller. Can you guess where this is going? The man never received his car, and e-mails to the escrow service went unanswered.

An escrow service is usually used for expensive goods — anywhere from $500 to $1000 on up. The benefit of using a legitimate escrow service is that the company acts as a neutral party to the transaction — the middle man, who protects both the buyer and the seller in case something goes wrong, and of course charges a fee for this service.

Online escrow fraud is fairly sophisticated. Con men copy information about real cars for sale on sites like AutoTrader.com and CACars.com, list them for sale on auction sites like eBay, and advise the buyer to wire money to them via a seemingly legitimate escrow service. It can go the other way, too: you can sell an item to a seemingly legitimate buyer, and send the goods after an escrow service notifies you that payment has been received, and then be out both payment and the item.

There are Web sites that track scam escrow sites: **www.sos4auctions.com**, for example, which lists over 100 fraudulent escrow sites. **www.CarBuyingTips.com** estimates that 90 percent of escrow Web sites are fake. But there are some helpful guidelines to avoid becoming their next victim.

One online shopper who is still bitter about the experience — he lost $3,000 in a fake escrow fiasco — says he will return to the world of Internet bidding. Why? Well, he recently found a Web site that proved...soothing.

"It's called **www.eBayersthatsuck.com**," he says (it was founded by a New Jersey cop who felt he was ripped off and lets the newly scammed tell their tales of woe in more than just the 80 characters that eBay provides for feedback), "And I bought something online from it."

What could possibly make a guy who lost three grand feel better? An official "eBayers that Suck Voodoo Doll."[4]

Important Tips

> Keep your personal information private. Don't disclose your address, telephone number, Social Security number or e-mail address unless you know who's collecting the information, why they're collecting it and how they'll use it. If you have children, teach them to check with you before giving out personal — or family — information online.

> The same is true in the bricks and mortar world. That fishbowl in the mall where you drop an entry form — do you know how the information you just voluntarily gave is going to be used?

> Look for a company's online privacy policy. Companies with privacy policies are required to post their privacy practices on their Web site. If you can't find a policy, send an e-mail or written message to the Web site to ask or consider shopping somewhere else.

> Shop with companies you know. If you're not familiar with a merchant, ask for a paper catalog or brochure to get a better idea of their merchandise and services. Also, determine the company's refund and return policies before you place your order.

> Make sure the Web site uses security software by checking for the following:

   - Your browser displays the icon of a locked padlock at the bottom of the screen (Netscape Navigator: versions 4.0 and higher);

   - You see the icon of an unbroken key at the bottom of the screen (earlier versions of Netscape Navigator);

   - You see the icon of a lock on the status bar (Microsoft Internet Explorer).

> Many Web merchants allow you to order online and give your credit card information over the phone. Make a note of the date and time of your call and the name of the person who took your call.

> Pay by credit or charge card. Your transaction will be protected by the Fair Credit Billing Act. Under this law, consumers can dispute charges under certain circumstances and temporarily withhold payment while the creditor is investigating them. In the event of unauthorized use of your credit or charge card, you are generally held liable only for the first $50 in charges. Some companies offer an online shopping guaran-

tee that ensures you will not be held responsible for *any* unauthorized charges made online, and some cards may provide additional warranty, return and/or purchase protection benefits.

> Pick one credit card for all your online purchases. Find a card that exempts you from the $50 liability charge.

> Be very careful about responding to an e-mail, phone call, fax or letter from *anyone* who asks for your password(s), social security number, birth date, bank account, credit card number, mother's maiden name or other personal information. To verify that the person contacting you really does work for the merchant, call the company and request to speak to that person directly.

> Use an escrow service recommended by the auction site (eBay suggests **www.escrow.com**). Fraudulent sites often mimic the names of real sites.

> Be wary if a seller insists on using a specific escrow site. Sellers don't usually press for escrow; buyers do.

> If you have been scammed on the Internet, contact the IFCC, which is a partnership between the FBI and the National White Collar Crime Center, at **www.ifccfbi.gov**.

 Let's Talk

These questions will help you, your family and others to begin a discussion about issues covered in this chapter.

1. What kind of background check, if any, do people on the online dating site you visit have to pass? Do I want to continue to use the site if they do nothing to ensure a person is who they claim to be?

2. Am I asking the right questions of people I meet online?

3. Am I providing too much information — too soon — making myself open to fraud?

4. When shopping online, do we know the merchant or site is legitimate? Do we know how to tell if the connection is secure? Do we use a credit card to pay for our online purchases?

5. Do we know the privacy policy of the merchant? Do we know how they are going to use the information we provide and if it will be shared with or sold to other merchants?

CHAPTER 4: **Medical Data and You**
From House Call to Web Call —
Computer, Heal Thyself!

New York Urologist Jeffrey Lavinge specialized in laser
surgery to remove warts and hemorrhoids. But what those
who entered his office didn't know was that more than 60
patients had sued Dr. Lavinge for botching their surgeries.
The Hartford Courant newspaper ran an exposé in 2000,
but not before Lavinge lost his license to practice medicine. An average person seeking information on the doctor
could not see the records the paper eventually uncovered.
And they still can't see all of them.

This is a nightmare scenario, but one that increasingly
can be avoided if you know where to look for medical
information and how to understand what you find.

Let's talk about the information that's out there.

When it comes to healthcare, it is plentiful. But how
accurate is it and who should have access to it? And
who ensures that information remains secure within the
medical establishment?

So Simple, So Logical

Certainly insurance companies, health plans and hospitals have a proprietary interest in some information — error rates for some treatments, for example. Who owns medical data is a major question that experts agree needs to be worked out. But the fact that the discussion is occurring on a national level is considered to be a breakthrough, and a positive one at that.

Many political and medical leaders are clamoring for a national electronic network of data that will allow patients and doctors to make better, more informed choices. For instance, a woman diagnosed with breast cancer or a man with chronic arthritis could tap into a database, where they would learn about others who consent to share information and who suffer from the same conditions. They could learn, for instance, what treatments worked (or didn't).

"The information is out there — we need to collect it and share it so it is useful," says Joe Kanter, a 79-year-old developer and cancer survivor who has led a six-year crusade to establish a national database. Kantor has put his money where his mouth is; his Kantor Foundation formed a partnership with the federal Agency for Healthcare Research and Quality.[1]

Supporters include former senators Bob Dole (R-Kansas) and George Mitchell (D-Maine), as well as current senate majority leader Bill Frist (R-Tenn.), who is also a physician. Mitchell called it an idea "so simple, so logical and so powerful in its implementation that it boggles the mind our society has not done this before now."

There already exists a National Practitioner Database funded by the federal government. But it is NOT currently open to the public (although other health care providers and the news media can access it as the Hartford Courant did). It contains a lot of very detailed information about doctors and how they do their jobs, but that's one reason why opening it to public scrutiny remains controversial.

"We Have an Illness!"

A recent RAND study found that patients — as well as doctors — want reliable information comparing treatment "outcomes." However, the study continues, patients are forced to "make difficult decisions every day with little or poor information to inform those choices." The RAND study estimated that each database for a disease or condition could cost $5 million to $10 million a year to standardize records and keep them updated.[2]

The Internet can be empowering when it comes to health care. Recent surveys show that up to 20 million U.S. adults researched medical or health related information online within the past year. But there are many issues with this, such as bogus treatments and self-medication through unregulated online pharmacies, which usually prey on those suffering terminal illnesses, the most vulnerable to false promises.

However, there is an undeniable advantage to being able to learn more about a particular ailment just by tapping a few words into a search engine. This is exactly what John Webster, a program director at Dakota State University in South Dakota did when he discovered small blisters on his head.

He used Ask.com to find out what was wrong with him. The diagnosis: "Dermatitis — dry itchy skin, which may result in scales or blisters," Webster writes on his Weblog, "All right! We have an illness!"[3]

That is, until he went to the next hit, which diagnosed his condition as plantar psoriasis, which may blister. All right! A second diagnosis! Next step: Webster turned to the medical sites for confirmation. "I tried a variety of health sites, including www.webmd.com, www.healthanswers.com, www.drkoop.com and www.mayohealth.org. These are great health sites, but none of them let me play doctor and diagnose myself. Instead, I could only search through specific areas of illnesses and conditions. Bitterness consumed me. The next day, I woke with moderate pain and discomfort. My small blisters had grown to large blisters and had spread beyond their original location."

Webster decided it was time to seek actual medical help and his physician diagnosed him with shingles. He returned to the Internet to learn more about shingles, but when his condition flared up the following day, Webster did not dally with Web surfing.

"Instead, I called my doctor and begged for drugs," he writes. "Then as fast as my short little legs would carry me, I scurried to the hospital to get them. The bottom line to all this? The Internet has some great medical sites where you can find lots of great information, but no matter how much you are tempted, don't let the Web take the place of your own doctor."

> The Internet has some great medical sites where you can find lots of great information, but no matter how much you are tempted, don't let the Web take the place of your own doctor.

Physicians themselves advise the same thing, although you might expect as much. Unsatisfactory consultations with medical professionals — and the undeniable convenience of the Internet — usually drive people to the Web for medical help. But, generic search engines offer only basic assistance, and doctors caution that even hospital and other health sites should emphasize the inappropriateness of self-diagnosis using Internet-acquired information.

One thing you SHOULD do, however, is keep track of your own medical information. One of the things about our mobile society is that you very likely have medical records scattered across several cities or states. How many different doctors have you been to in the last few years? All of that information should be in one place for instant, easy access. You should keep a medical file on yourself. Every time you go to the doctor, keep a record of your visit, the diagnosis and the medication prescribed. And then put this information in a safe place. This is all especially important if you have children.

This will help doctors provide the best possible treatment in the future. If you don't keep the records, make sure someone does it for you and can get to them in an emergency.

Important Tips

> Contact your personal doctors and ask if they will allow you to have copies of your own medical records.

> Ask questions of potential health care providers. If you are not satisfied with the answers, keep pushing. Too many people hesitate to demand clear answers to the life and death questions regarding health care.

> These sites offer great research on medical conditions and treatments: **www.nlm.nih.gov/databases/databases_medline.html** — United States National Library of Medicine site for tens of thousands of medical journal articles. And **www.cancer.gov** provides information on cancer. Web sites like **www.webmd.com** and **www.mayo.org** offer a wealth of information and resources. Check the Web site of your local hospital or medical provider, too.

The Doctor Will See You Now

Choosing the right hospital or doctor matters, of course. A recent report by the Institute of Medicine found that up to 98,000 Americans die every year from preventable errors made in hospitals. For some high-risk procedures, such as heart surgery, which studies have shown more than three times the difference in surgical mortality rates across hospitals, the choice of where to have such procedures may mean the difference, literally, between life and death.

On a Web site run by an independent state agency in Pennsylvania, Dr. Ron D. Nutting, from West Reading, comes up as a top heart surgeon.

As part of an effort to address escalating health costs and ensure quality care, the Pennsylvania Health Care Cost Containment Council publishes an online box score that lists doctors who performed coronary artery bypass grafts: **www.phc4.org**.

The agency posts the doctor-by-doctor listing after culling through two million inpatient discharge records it collects each year. Visitors to the Web site can check on a specific hospital's performance, based on risk-adjusted mortality rates.

Nutting's numbers paint a picture of a doctor who is not only experienced, but also skilled.

In the 155 bypass procedures performed in the year in question, the number of Nutting's patients who died during surgery was "as expected," according to the Web site while the number who needed to be readmitted to the hospital was "lower than expected."

Despite his excellent numbers, Nutting says the rankings don't tell the whole story. Because most of the doctor ratings are based on discharge records (or what is basically accounting information), and not risk analysis, Dr. Nutting believes doctors may not receive fair assessments. The bottom line, he says, is these Web sites can be somewhat helpful, but he warns there is not enough quality information out there for the patient to always make an informed choice.

That is key to an understanding of the situation. And it isn't easy. Different states, hospitals, doctors, boards and companies collect and dispense different types of information. It is ultimately up to you to try to understand exactly what the reports and statistics you find measure and what they don't.

To that end, some organizations are working hard to provide more guidance to help you make better choices.

The Business Roundtable, an organization of corporations and corporate leaders, founded the Leapfrog Group (www.leapfroggroup.org) to track the safety of health care. This voluntary program has collected data in 22 regions, accounting for nearly half of the U.S. population. There is also the Joint Commission on Accreditation of Healthcare Organizations, an independent, non-profit that evaluates quality and safety of care for more than 16,000 health care organizations, which offers performance reviews of hospitals through its Web site **www.jcaho.org**.

Estimates show that from one to three percent of doctors have had sanctions or disciplinary actions filed against them. These are especially tough to track. For instance, if a doctor has been disciplined in one state, like Iowa, but is licensed to practice in several states, the Web sites for other state medical boards will not include the Iowa action. And, sanctions don't necessarily mean a physician is prevented from practicing.

An Iowa anesthesiologist who fell asleep during surgery and then left the operating room during surgery and falsified records was suspended for a month, fined $5,000 and placed on five years of probation. He is still practicing. Another Iowa doctor, who performed excessive, unnecessary or inappropriate surgery and engaged in a sexual relationship with a patient, had his license suspended but then reinstated with probation. These are just two of the estimated 20,000 doctors nationwide who have been disciplined.[4]

Dr. Sidney Wolfe, the director of Public Citizen's Health Research Program, says: "People are finding out things about their doctors that raise questions," says Wolfe. "They can then make more informed decisions. Unfortunately, most states are doing a poor job of disciplining their doctors, so it is often up to individuals to learn as much as they can on their own."

Important Tips

> Contact your state department of health to learn what doctor and hospital databases are available online.

> ChoicePoint offers license and sanction information on doctors, nurses, dentists and chiropractors at **www.choicetrust.com**. Basic information is free; detailed reports are available for a nominal charge. Write in the name of the provider to learn more about the person.

> Similar services are available from Healthgrades (**www.healthgrades.com**) and Public Citizen offers physician information for sale at **www.questionabledoctors.org**.

> Physician profiles, including education, training, specialty, malpractice and disciplinary proceedings, are available in California, Florida, Idaho, Massachusetts, New York, Oregon, Rhode Island and

Washington State. A link to the state sites can be found at
www.healthcarechoices.org/profile.htm.

> At least 18 states now place information online about doctors and
hospitals, although it is not always easy to find and the data is sometimes at least five years old. Check with your state health department
to find what information is available. But here are examples of what
some states provide:

  - New York has reports on angioplasty and coronary artery bypass
    surgery: **www.health.state.ny.us/nysdoh/heart/heart_disease.htm**.

  - Illinois posts costs per hospital for different procedures, and
    gives statistics about how hospitals handled births at the hospital,
    with information such as length of stay and the rate caesarean
    sections were performed:
    www.state.il.us/agency/hcccc/ConsumerReports.htm#survey00.

  - California lists heart attack and coronary artery bypass outcomes
    by hospital statewide, although the data is old:
    www.oshpd.cahwnet.gov/HQAD/reports.htm.

  - New Jersey posts a report listing hospital and surgeon performance
    for cardiac surgery:
    www.state.nj.us/health/hcsa/cabgs01/cabg_technical01.pdf.

Just Say No to Drugs (Advertising)

Public Citizen maintains a pharmaceutical database, which lists the
160 drugs that some organizations claim are too dangerous to use
at **www.worstpills.org** (of course, the drug companies and many
doctors disagree.)

But what Dr. Wolfe really worries about is instant access to Internet
medicine and drug ads on the Web.

You may not know what you are getting, since many of the companies
are not reputable. A recent study by the University of Pennsylvania found
86 Web sites selling sildenafil — more commonly known as Viagra —
without a doctor's visit or a prescription. More than one-quarter of these
sites were based outside the United States. And, an undercover investigation in the state of Kansas revealed that some companies knowingly sold
sildenafil to 16-year-olds.[5]

Dr. Wolfe, adds, "We say people should pay no attention to ads for prescription drugs."

In this age of self-diagnosis, he says, "overstating the benefits and understating the risks is quite common. It's difficult to sort out information that is correct from information that isn't correct. People die from misleading information."

Important Tips

> You should always consult your doctor before purchasing medication online or taking any drugs, even seemingly innocuous herbal remedies.

> If you purchase drugs online, use only services a health care professional or your insurance company has recommended.

> Never buy prescriptions from services you have only learned about via e-mail.

> Never assume solicitations to purchase drugs online are truthful without doing your due diligence.

Checking Up on Nursing Homes

One of the fastest growing segments of health care is long-term care facilities, otherwise known as nursing homes. Currently, there are 1.5 million Americans in nursing homes. As the U.S. population ages, more and more Americans will face the difficult decision of placing their parents — and even themselves — in a nursing home. The standards of care can vary widely. A recent,

in-depth investigation by Gannett News Service found that nearly three-fourths of the most severe and repeated nursing home patient care violations were concentrated in a dozen states. And, patients at homes owned by for-profit companies actually fared worse, in some ways, than residents in government or nonprofit nursing homes.[6]

The study found that patients in for-profit homes had higher rates of infections and pressure sores than those owned by the government and nonprofit organizations. These are things that are not necessarily measured by the Web site set up by the federal government to monitor nursing homes and to provide more information about them. Be careful to evaluate each home separately.

Anne Smith, a nurse in Salt Lake City, told Gannet reporters that when she needed to find a nursing home for her 88-year-old mother, who was recovering from a heart ailment, a hospital discharge planner handed her a list of 31 nursing homes in the area. Smith relied on the federal government's Nursing Home Compare Web site **(http://www.medicare.gov/NHCompare/home. asp)**, which lists residents' health status and inspection results for all Medicare- and Medicaid-certified nursing homes.

The government spent about $30 million to draw attention to this Web project, and it features inspection and patient health results for every nursing home in the country. With a list of nursing homes from the Web site, Smith narrowed her choices and made a selection. "[The Web site] helped me go to a nursing home and ask them, 'What is your strategy for caring for my mother, because you don't look very good on paper'," Smith told the news service.

Important Tips

> Check out the following Web sites for detailed information on long-term and nursing home care:

   www.memberofthefamily.net

   www.nursinghomereports.com

   www.carescout.com

   www.choicetrust.com

Keeping Medical Matters Private

One final note on the issue of medical privacy. The Health Insurance Portability and Accountability Act (HIPAA) set a national standard for medical privacy by making the unauthorized release of medical information a crime. Lawmakers wanted to allow patients easier access to their medical records and to limit others' ability to get to such information.

Interpreting the privacy provision has led to complications that no one really predicted. For example, thousands of doctors have stopped sending out appointment-reminder postcards; someone other than the patient could theoretically read the cards. And some doctors have stopped leaving messages on patients' telephone answering machines for the same reason, and spouses have been told they can no longer verify

- The Health Insurance Portability and Accountability Act (HIPAA) set a national standard for medical privacy by making the unauthorized release of medical information a crime.

dental appointments for their husbands or wives. Some hospitals stopped providing information to patients' family members and clergy, and some weekly newspapers no longer publish birth announcements (hospitals stopped providing the names).

These are extreme interpretations. The law does not prohibit hospitals from providing names and basic information on patients. Call your health care providers to learn what their privacy policies are. As with every other topic discussed in this book, the responsibility to learn more about medical privacy and how it could impact you or your family members falls squarely on your shoulders.

Despite all these complicated and developing issues, technology is changing the face of healthcare in positive ways. But it is important to remember: you can research your condition, increase your knowledge of medical issues and even attempt to diagnose yourself, but that does not make you a doctor. Understand your limits and always consult with your physician.

 Let's Talk

These questions will help you, your family and others to begin a discussion about issues covered in this chapter.

1. Have we researched our family health care providers, including our doctors, dentists, chiropractors and home care nurses? What's the best way for us to learn more about health care providers?

2. Where can we learn more about diseases or disorders that our doctor has discussed with us?

3. Have we researched our hospitals and nursing homes to learn more about the quality of care at the facilities?

4. Have we asked our doctor or insurance company about the benefits and pitfalls of ordering medicine over the Internet?

5. Do we know what our rights are under the new medical privacy law, HIPAA?

CHAPTER 5: **Protection from Predators**
Keeping Your Children Safe

Predators Online

Julie Posey has made the Internet safe for the name "Kendra."

The police officer in Wellington, Kansas, has been visiting chat rooms and other areas on the Internet, pretending to be a 13- or 14-year-old girl named Kendra; a lonely, vulnerable teen who has proven to be irresistible to pedophiles. "Kendra" has received all sorts of communications from these guys: requests for nude photos, child pornography and invitations to meet up.

Posey's undercover work has resulted in 68 arrests and a 100 percent conviction rate. She now has a reputation for effectiveness; and, "girls across the U.S. named Kendra should be safe," Posey laughs. It is one bright, light moment amid work that is undeniably dark.

Around 25 million American children are using the Internet. One out of five of them have been solicited for sex! One in four have been sent photos of people who were naked or having sex. And an estimated 725,000 children have been aggressively asked for sex, with an invitation to meet their predators face-to-face.

Here are more numbers to send a chill through you: there are 400,000 registered sex offenders in the U.S.; 58 percent of those are out in the community, as opposed to being locked up in prison. And 70 percent of them are on the Internet, lurking behind the guise of a friendly, understanding, attentive young man (most pedophiles start out saying they are 21, according to Posey, when they are actually 35 or older).

In Boca Raton, Florida, a respected 59-year-old rabbi pleaded guilty to two counts of soliciting sex from a minor. Prosecutors say that Gerald Levy prowled chat rooms, asking teenage boys for nude photos and phone sex. A prominent Internet executive, Patrick Naughton, pleaded guilty to traveling from his home in Seattle to southern California to meet a 13-year-old girl he had been corresponding with on-line. And, it isn't just men who are the perpetrators. Gloria Jean Farrell had a yearlong e-mail exchange with a 13-year-old boy, whom she lured from his North Carolina home and drove him to Alabama where for 12 days she had sex with him, did drugs with him and drank with him[2]

"I think parents should be very worried," Posey says. "There are a lot of risks on the Internet. Kids generally put way too much personal and identifying information on the Internet, and whatever void is in their life, [the pedophile] is there to fill it."

Katherine Tarbox was 13 when she met 23-year-old "Mark" in an online chat room. A top student and nationally ranked swimmer attending an elite school in an affluent Connecticut town, Katie was also a lonely and self-conscious eighth-grader (who isn't at that age?) and she craved the attention her workaholic parents couldn't give her. "Mark," however, seemed to understand her; he told her she was smart and wonderful. After six months of communicating, they set a date to finally meet while Katie was in Texas for a school swim competition. She walked into a hotel room and discovered who — and what — her cyber soul mate really was. "Our lips met," she writes in her book, *Katie.com*. "I felt a few stray whiskers... and suddenly I realized that this was a grown man who was giving me my first real kiss... Something inside me snapped. Now I didn't want this at all. But I couldn't speak."

"Mark" was actually Frank Kufrovich, a man in his forties with a history of pedophilia. Katie decided to write *Katie.com* so that other teens might avoid a similar situation. Indeed, Katie was manipulated and molested, but she fought back by prosecuting Kufrovich under the Communications Decency Act of 1996. She considered herself to be one of the "lucky" ones.

"Thirteen or 14 is like the magic number for pedophiles," Posey says. "When they see there's a 13-year-old in the chat room, they swarm. I will get 20 to 40 contacts in the first five minutes of posing as a 13-year-old. They're not saying 'Hey, how are you?' They're saying, 'Are you a virgin?' or 'Are you sure you're 13? I like 13-year-olds'."

Chat rooms are an even more dangerous place than parents might realize. Many allow kids to hook up a Web cam. Pedophiles will then try to talk children into stripping.

Even Web sites that service millions without a problem can unintentionally provide a tool for pedophiles. For example, a predator can find a child's "wish list" on popular Web sites. They will then contact children and tell them that they know a way for the child to get everything on their list.

Then, there are the favorite ways kids use the Internet: instant messaging, peer-to-peer connections, and sharing MP3 music files. All of these allow strangers with less-than-honest intentions to contact children.

The Internet, vast and cold and prowled by predators, may seem impossible to control. It might be easy to think, "I'll just keep my kids offline entirely." Not exactly a practical tactic.

Protecting Your Children

There are ways to fight back. For instance, ComputerCOP, a free CD-Rom program developed by former New York City police officer Bo Dietl (**www.computercop.com**), gathers all photo files on a computer's hard drive and scans text documents (including e-mails and chat room exchanges) for more than 1,000 red-flag words. These words include sexual and drug and weapons terms, and also words that are known to be used by pedophiles and cyberstalkers. For example, one word often used by pedophiles is "uncle." Once the files are compiled, parents can search through them easily. ComputerCOP boots directly from the CD-ROM. Users are not required to load it into their computers permanently.

Posey advises parents, "If you have to get software to supervise your kids on the Internet, do it." There are programs like Spectresoft, which Posey herself uses (it gives her a real-time copy of the sites her daughter visits on the Internet and every message she sends or receives), and Net Nanny, which limits what sites you can visit. AOL offers its Guardian Service via its 9.0 edition.

One easy step is to put the computer in a common area of the house. Kids should not be on the Internet behind closed doors, and parents should make sure that their children do not password protect their computers. This is because pedophiles will teach kids how to password protect the computer and how to wipe out files showing who they have communicated with.

> Kids should not be on the Internet behind closed doors, and parents should make sure that their children do not password protect their computers.

"Pedophiles really want to talk to kids on the phone," Posey says. "They will try to get the kid's number, and if that fails, they will e-mail the kid a prepaid phone card. Or, they'll arrange to send the kid things via general delivery at the local post office. Parents need to be aware of where gifts like phones and video games are coming from."

If you suspect your child is communicating online with a sexual predator, you should immediately talk (and talk openly) with your child about your suspicions, and tell them about the dangers of such communications. Next, review what is on your child's computer. Pornography or any kind of sexual communication can be a red flag. Order Caller ID service from your phone company to determine who is calling your child. This will help prevent someone from calling your house anonymously. Most telephone companies that offer Caller ID also offer a blocking service to prevent your number from showing up on someone else's Caller ID. Telephone companies also offer an additional service feature that rejects incoming calls from numbers you choose to block.

Monitor your child's access to all types of live communications (chat rooms, instant messages, etc.). You also should immediately contact your local or state law enforcement agency, the FBI (www.fbi.gov) and the Center for Missing and Exploited Children (www.missingkids.com) if you suspect your child has been contacted by a pedophile.

If someone who knows your child is under 18 sexually solicits them (or sends them pornography), turn the computer off. This will preserve any evidence for future law enforcement use. Unless directed to do so by the law enforcement agency, do not copy any of the images or text found on the computer (to avoid any possibility of you being accused of possessing pornography).

Important Tips

> Set up rules for your child's computer use and follow them. Monitor your own child's time online and check things out if it seems the child is logged on excessively or if the hours are odd or secretive. Make sure your children understand they should never give out personal information online. Maintain an open dialogue with your child. Don't play the blame game; encourage honest discussion about what a child has seen or done on the Internet.

> Sit down with your children and join them on the Internet. Ask what your children's friends do when they are online.

> Respect your children's concerns or frustrations over your involvement in their surfing activities.

> Alert your Internet Service Provider to any inappropriate e-mails.

> Check out www.Pedowatch.com, which is run by Julie Posey and has tips on how to prevent child sexual abuse.

> Check out www.Cybertipline.com, which is operated by the National Center for Missing & Exploited Children and handles leads from individuals reporting the sexual exploitation of children.

> Check out www.NetSafeKids.org, which includes information on everything from guidelines for creating Internet use agreements for children to a discussion of legal and First Amendment issues of Internet pornography.

> Delete inappropriate or X-rated mail and do not respond to it.

> Check the history of your child's Internet browsers often. Check your child's downloads folder in their Home folder. If the folder has been removed from the desktop, you will find it in the Documents folder.

> Set a rule that your child never arranges an in-person meeting with someone you don't know without you present.

Stalkers Online

It is not just pedophiles that you need to be concerned about on the Internet; the anonymity of the World Wide Web has given rise to a whole new crime: *cyberstalking*. It can happen to anyone — children, adults, men, and women. And this is very tricky, because arrests are rare.

Upwards of 100 new cases of *cyberstalking*, someone using the Internet to intimidate another person, are reported each week. Colin Hatcher, president of SafetyEd, one of the few private groups that help victims of Internet stalking, told the *Christian Science Monitor* that "probably two-thirds involve revenge; someone loses an argument or is turned down romantically."

But although lawmakers and police readily acknowledge the seriousness of the problem, they admit that more pressing offenses often cause them to overlook a crime that can be time-consuming and difficult to prosecute. Stalking is never an easy case; the global nature of the Internet means that the culprit could live in another state or even country. Extradition isn't likely for what is usually regarded as a misdemeanor.

However, file a police report anyway. Many times, cyberstalkers will stop after receiving even one quick communication from a law enforcement agency.

Important Tips

> Contact groups like SafetyEd (**www.safetyed.org**), Working to Halt Online Abuse (WHOA) (**www.haltabuse.org**) and Wired Patrol (**www.wiredpatrol.org**)
>
> Their Web sites offer advice to Internet users, including having one e-mail address for chat rooms and maintaining another, private address for friends.

> Contact your local police and the above organizations when you are being harassed. Stalkers often stop once police or private agencies come to them with evidence tying them to threatening messages.

Pornography Online

Sometimes, it's not WHO enters your children's life, but WHAT enters their lives.

There is an onslaught of sexually explicit material on the Web. It may not be sent to your child by an online predator, but it is easily available — and often free. Adult-oriented sites make up less than 2 percent of all Internet content, but that fraction is highly visible and accounts for an amazing amount of Web traffic.

The adult online entertainment industry rakes in about $1 billion a year in revenue and it's growing; U.S.-based businesses support about 100,000 sites, while globally there are about 400,000 adult, for-profit sites.[3] According to a recent Nielsen/Net Ratings report, nearly 16 percent of visitors to adult-oriented sites were under the age of 18. And, the most graphic image can make its way onto a child's computer screen without being actively sought.

Technologies that screen for spam can miss some pornographic e-mails. Spam can contain embedded links to explicitly sexual material, which are often overlooked by these tools.

The National Academy of Science reports that there is no simple way to protect children from Internet porn. The best strategy is a combination of social and educational interventions, technology-based tools and legal and regulatory approaches.

Important Tips

> Parents, teachers, librarians and other adult supervisors can find a comprehensive guide to consumer products for monitoring Internet usage, filtering unwanted content or controlling computer use on **GetNetWise.org**. "GetNetWise" is an industry-public partnership aimed at educating kids and families on how to have safe, rewarding, online experiences.

> Age verification technologies try to differentiate between adults and children in an online environment. For example, sites can request a valid credit card number before granting users access to the site. Unfortunately, this tactic will become less effective as more children begin to use credit cards.

> Newer verification tools are becoming more widely available that require a person to answer questions only they would know how to correctly answer, greatly reducing the chances of a child impersonating their parent or other adult.

> Filters are the most widely used tool; three-fourths of U.S. schools use some kind of blocking or filtering software. These can be highly effective, but they also can block an enormous amount of educational and informative content. A recent study by the Kaiser Family Foundation showed that nearly half of

teens seeking online health information were blocked from sites that were not pornographic.

Beware of Strangers

Keeping potentially damaging segments of the "virtual" world away from your family is hard enough.

Keeping potential 'real world' risks away can be equally tough.

"Beware of strangers" is one of the first and most specific lessons that parents teach their children. Of course, "strangers" aren't just clever e-mailers floating through the World Wide Web; we run into "strangers" every day — they deliver our pizzas, run local basketball programs, even cut our lawns.

And this last one might remind you of a particularly horrible crime: the abduction of a 15-year-old girl from her home by a man who had been hired by the family to do handy work. This is, of course, the case of Elizabeth Smart, who was eventually returned to her family. But the incident sent ripples of terror across the country. Ed Smart was just trying to do a good deed in hiring a down-and-out man to do some yard work, and look what happened.

The lesson is: do your due diligence. Find out about the people who work in your home and care for your children and other loved ones.

Important Tips

> Check with the National Center for Missing and Exploited Children (**www.missingkids.com**). Their Web site is filled with good advice on protecting your children.

> Do background checks on people who enter your home. One way is to use ChoicePoint's background check at **www.choicetrust.com**. For a fee, you can check or background screen people you hire, including home care workers, contractors, and house cleaners in a way that complies with privacy laws. Similar services are offered by **www.4nannies.com** and **www.USSearch.com**. See Chapter 6 for details on how to do background checks.

> Contact your local or state government consumer advocate to find out if your community requires licenses for contractors and home care workers. If they do, ask how you can verify a person's license.

> If you hire a person to work at your home through another business — like a home improvement or repair company — ask if they perform background checks on the employees or subcontractors sent to your home. If they say no, be prepared to find another service provider.

Keeping Schools and Volunteer Organizations Safer

A similar issue faces those who choose the people who teach your children and work in your community's volunteer organizations.

The background checks they perform can be incomplete.

Just as doctors who are sanction-free in one state may not have a good record in another, teachers who have been convicted in a state other than Illinois, for example, could still be hired by an Illinois school district.[4]

That's because Illinois is one of three states in the nation that do not require fingerprints or national background checks for educators. A teaching application is reviewed only for convictions within Illinois. According to a 2003 Chicago Tribune study, Bruce Kimball, a former Olympic diver, was convicted in 1989 of killing two people in a DUI manslaughter case that was national news. However, the case happened in Florida. When Kimball, whose case was widely publicized when it occurred, applied to be the diving coach at an Illinois high school, one of the best high schools in the country, "no record on file" flashed up during the background check. In another case, a principal, who was convicted of financial fraud in Wisconsin, was able to hide his federal prison record for two years.

It may seem like a no-brainer to fingerprint prospective teachers and other school employees and to run background checks, but the cost does add up. With fingerprints, a national criminal history search can be conducted through FBI records. The FBI search costs $24, and when a state police check and administrative fees are tacked on, the cost ranges from $45 to $55. Many people, though, would argue that no cost is too great when it comes to protecting the safety and well-being of their children.

In fact, fingerprinting is automatic in most states for teachers, and applications in a school district in Las Vegas ask teachers 13 questions about their criminal past; an Atlanta suburban district asks applicants if they have ever been investigated for discrimination or sexual harassment, regardless of the outcome of the case; and Florida districts require applicants to reveal juvenile convictions and expunged criminal records. All of this is considered too probing in Illinois, where state laws are written to protect the right to privacy.

So here's what you need to do.

Ask about your district's policy, ask what type of background screening they do and, if you aren't satisfied, press for change.

Volunteer organizations face similar questions.

There are screening programs designed especially to meet the needs of non-profit organizations. These programs are used to filter volunteers for the Boys and Girls Club of America, American Red Cross, U.S. Conference of Bishops, the Boy Scouts of America and U.S. Youth Soccer among others.

Statistics show a consistent three percent "hit" rate for undisclosed criminal convictions for volunteer applicants. They include not only serial pedophiles, but also people with a history of violence against children, and a large number of drug and alcohol offenses. This rate is better than the nine percent conviction rate seen in the general employment pool, but still higher than expected given the nature of people who volunteer.

Important Tips

> Ask companies who send people into your home and volunteer organizations if they perform background checks on the people who work for them. Ask them specifically if they performed a *criminal* background check.

> Many local and state police departments offer limited volunteer background checks that look for convictions within a community or state. ChoicePoint's VolunteerSelect (**www.volunteerselect.com**) is endorsed by the National Assembly of Health and Human Service Organizations and available to non-profit organizations at minimal costs who need a comprehensive background check.

A Safety Net for Your Child

Every parent's fear, of course, is that someone takes their child.

Exact numbers are hard to come by, but the second National Incidence Study of Missing, Abducted, Runaway and Throwaway Children counted more than 730,000 children reported "missing" in the most recent report. About 200,000 were taken by family members. Nearly 60,000 were taken by non-

- The second National Incidence Study of Missing, Abducted, Runaway and Throwaway Children counted more than 730,000 children reported "missing" in the most recent report. About 200,000 were taken by family members. Nearly 60,000 were taken by non-family members, but only 115 were the victims of actual stranger kidnappings.

family members, but only 115 were the victims of actual stranger kidnappings.

If you are a parent, it doesn't matter how your child went missing, only that they are. Most parents will never experience the pain of an abducted child, but you should still act like a Boy Scout: Be Prepared.

Later, in chapter eight, we'll explore how you can harness the power of DNA, the fingerprint for this century, to help protect your children.

Important Tips

Here is a list of the things you need to have handy in the event of an emergency involving your child:

> A recent photograph (the most important element), preferably a digital photo for easy distribution by police officers.

> Dental chart.

> Complete personal information including the child's name, address and Social Security number.

> The names and phone numbers of family and friends.

> Medical information such as blood type, medications and phone numbers of the child's doctor and dentist.

> Updated physical information, including height, weight, eye color and hair color.

> Fingerprinting chart done by a law enforcement official.

> A copy of your child's birth certificate. You can order an expedited copy from the government agency that issued the certificate through ChoicePoint's VitalChek system online at **www.vitalchek.com** or by calling **1-866-322-8822**.

Not taking the time to do these simple tasks can lead to a harsh lesson: one that John and Magi Bish unfortunately learned.

Their 16-year-old daughter, Molly, disappeared one bright summer day in 2000 from the sandy shore of a small town pond in Massachusetts. When the Bishes were asked to provide Molly's photo for a Missing Person poster, they realized they did not have an appropriate photo ready. They had plenty of prom photos (with Molly in a fancy "up" hair-do that was not her usual look) and outdated, professional-quality photographs. Magi Bish needed to crop several group photographs in order to produce a picture of Molly in her most recent short haircut.

Any tool that saves time is critical to the safe recovery of a missing child. Another hard lesson for the Bishes — fingerprints. They did not have a set of Molly's fingerprints to give to police in the hours after her disappearance. Instead, the police had to come to the house and lift prints from Molly's room: a time-consuming process that is not as effective as a set of clean, professionally made fingerprints.

Then, the summer of 2003, in the woods off West Warren Road in Palmer, only five miles from the pond and her family's home, Molly Bish's remains were found. She was buried on what would have been her twentieth birthday.

Her family maintains a Web site (**www.mollybish.org**) dedicated both to finding her abductor and helping other families protect their children.

There is also this poignant reminder of the loss felt by the Bish family.

"Christopher Robin?," whispered Pooh.
"Yes, Pooh Bear?"
"I'll never not remember you... ever."

Let's Talk

These questions will help you, your family and others to begin a discussion about issues covered in this chapter.

1. What sites do our family members visit?

2. Have we discussed what computer uses are acceptable? Is our computer located in an appropriate location?

3. Do we have the appropriate software installed to block inappropriate material and to monitor inappropriate uses?

4. Do the organizations our family participates in conduct criminal background checks on employees and volunteers? If not, what would it take to start conducting background screens? Do we want to continue in the group if they refuse?

5. Do we have a home ID kit for each family member, especially our children?

CHAPTER 6: **Check, Verify and Validate**
Protecting Your Family

Jerrold Woods was one of those guys who you would never *invite* into your own home. At 52, he had racked up nine armed robberies and ten years in prison. But there he was, walking into Kerry Spooner Dean's house in the San Francisco Bay Area. She even held the door open for him. The pediatrician was not aware of Woods' frightening history. She thought he was there to clean her carpets.

Many companies, like America's Best Carpet Cleaner, do not run background checks on employees. Some industries, like those that provide home services, inevitably take on employees with criminal backgrounds. A pizza delivery man in Nebraska, who had been jailed 16 times, including once for sexual assault, raped a woman after delivering a pizza to her house. He is currently serving a 25-30 year jail term, but that company still does not require its franchise owners to do criminal background checks. A man who cleaned carpets for a well-known company in Maryland — and had a long, unchecked criminal record — sexually assaulted a woman in her home. And then, there is what happened to 30-year-old Kerry Spooner Dean, who unlocked her door for Jerrold Woods and was viciously stabbed to death.

Dean's husband, Daniel, filed a wrongful death lawsuit against the carpet cleaning company and won a $9.38 million judgment against the company. No money was actually ever paid out — the company had dissolved by then — but that wasn't really the point. "We wanted to send a message to small businesses," says Spooner's mother, Mary. "Before my daughter's death, I didn't think twice about trades people coming into my home. Now, I ask if companies do background checks on their employees. Many businesses find this an unusual question."

You can't count on companies or even the government to always screen. There are so many risks coming from so many areas that some measure of personal responsibility is needed — both by you and by the businesses you rely on.

One thing has been proven by the tragic death of Kerry Spooner Dean: companies that provide home services that do not do background checks of their employees are running huge financial risks. "A company is more likely to go out of business if they get hit with something like that," says Jeff Bishop, the administrator of Clean Care Seminars, Inc., who also advises any small business that sends employees into customers' homes to do background checks. "Employees should be screened for criminal background information and for drugs."

"The cost for background checks is nominal," adds Paul Scott, who was the attorney for Daniel Dean. "After our verdict was publicized, the home service industry reacted to some extent, but many firms have gone back to their old ways. I think there is simply a tendency for businesses to think it can't happen to them."

Screening Service People

Business executives aren't the only ones who should look at a job applicant's history. So should you. You will want to do background checks on individuals you bring into your home — workers such as nannies, housekeepers, gardeners, etc.

First, you must make the decision whether you want to perform the check yourself or hire someone to do it for you. If you do it yourself, you need to understand that you will not have access to some information that may be valuable to you, such as a person's credit history or, in most states, a person's driving record.

And you must obtain the permission of the applicant BEFORE you begin to conduct your research to ensure you protect their privacy.

Knowing all that, there are a number of online resources that can help you.

You can verify addresses and published telephone numbers online.

You can find criminal conviction histories online in some states, including separate listings of convicted sexual offenders.

You can also visit your local courthouse to see if an applicant has been the subject of a criminal or civil case.

Regardless of the source, on or offline, inquire about how frequently the information is updated and if the information available will help you make a good decision.

Arrest records are generally not used by reputable background screening companies. Only convictions are generally considered reflective of a person's true behavior.

If you hire someone to do the background research and you decide, based on the research, not to hire an applicant, the information must be shared with that person so that they have a chance to point out inaccuracies or misleading information. That's not just being nice, that's required by the federal Fair Credit Reporting Act.

If you do the background check yourself, it is less clear whether you must share the information. But good privacy practices dictate that you should.

Several companies offer products that will check out anyone you are hiring on a one-to-one payment basis: carpet cleaner, dog walker, babysitter. Depending upon what you want to find out, for between $25 and $99, those companies will search national criminal files, country criminal files, motor vehicle reports and more. A search can only happen with the consent of the individual.

If someone questions the check, you can say, "We screen everybody who comes into

Did You Know?

- Many small companies do not run background checks on employees.

- Business executives aren't the only ones who should look at a job applicant's history. So should you. You will want to do background checks on individuals you bring into your home — workers such as nannies, housekeepers, gardeners, etc.

- You must obtain the permission of the applicant BEFORE you begin to conduct your research to ensure you protect their privacy.

- If you hire someone to do the background research and you decide, based on the research, not to hire an applicant, the information must be shared with that person so they have a chance to point out inaccuracies or misleading information.

our home." If a person refuses, it's up to you to consider whether you wish to hire them anyway.

Such searches are confined to the job applicant who grants permission. You cannot, for instance, do a search on that annoying neighbor next door just because you are "curious."

After doing basic due diligence that verifies a person is who they claim to be, worked where they claimed to work and attended the schools they listed, you need to match the job duties of the applicant with the kind of information available that will help you make a decision. For example, if your employee is going to drive as part of their job duties, you need to review their driving record. If they are going to handle cash, you may want to request a credit report. (It might give you an indication of how they handle money.) If you want to be very thorough in searching for criminal records, you might even want to request a courthouse search where a person searches through original files to determine the circumstances of a criminal conviction.

It is important to keep in mind that you have to monitor your own risk and balance this with the right of those who have paid their debt to society, a.k.a. served time in jail. To forgive is fine; to forget may not be.

 Important Tips

Home Safety

> Most crimes occur when the resident is alone. Make sure there is more than one person in the home when workers are there.

> If you are alone, mention that a spouse or a friend is coming over.

> The best way to hire any type of service provider is to do due diligence. This includes talking to friends, neighbors and the Better Business Bureau. But it also means asking businesses for assurance that they run background checks on employees.

> If you are hiring individuals to work in your home (such as nannies, cooks, gardeners), you should take an extra step: do a background check.

Background Checks

> If you are going to hire a background screening company, you need to make sure they comply with state and federal privacy laws. To learn what your state requires, check with the state's Consumer Advocate or

State Attorney General's office. For Federal laws, check with the FTC (**www.ftc.gov**).

> Federal law and some state laws require a job applicant give their permission before a background check can be conducted. Applicants have additional rights if you decide not to hire them based on the information in the background check.

> Your background screening company should be able to help you comply with the applicable state and federal laws. If they can't, look for one that can.

> Small business owners can purchase inexpensive, but comprehensive background screening services through ChoicePoint's ScreenNow (**www.screennow.com**). Individuals can order privacy law compliant screening services for home care workers through ChoicePoint's ChoiceTrust.com (**www.choicetrust.com**). Similar services are available from USSearch.com and private investigators.

> If you're doing your own background check, you can verify basic public information (name, address, telephone number) through services like ChoicePoint's KnowX (**www.knowx.com**), AT&T's AnyWho (**www.anywho.com**), or major search engines like Yahoo! and Google. You can use KnowX to check other public records, including business licenses, liens, lawsuits and business bankruptcies (but not personal bankruptcies).

> Check **www.small-claims-court.net** to find a variety of small claims court records.

What to Do if You're the One Being Screened

If you apply for a job or a volunteer position, your prospective boss may run a background check on YOU.

It is most important for you to be honest.

Do not misstate or embellish. Studies show around two-thirds of all resumes have intentional errors. One-third of job applications have misleading information. I've already mentioned that some studies indicate 9% of job applicants have undisclosed criminal convictions.

The risk of being dishonest: Veritas Software Corp., in California, forced its chief financial officer to resign after learning he lied about his education, such as a Stanford University MBA that he never received. And Bausch &

Lomb, Inc. withheld a $1.1 million bonus that it had promised its chief executive, rather than accept his resignation for falsely claiming he had graduated from business school.

The Fair Credit Reporting Act gives you specific rights when your background is being checked. Under the FCRA:

> The employer must clearly disclose to the applicant, in a separate document, that a report is being prepared. The disclosure can no longer be buried in the "fine print" of an application.

> A signed release is required before checking records such as criminal convictions or pending criminal cases, driving records, credit reports or education credentials.

> Additional notice is required when a background check firm checks references, like asking previous employers about job performance.

> If an employer intends to deny employment based upon the background check, you must receive a copy of the report and a notice of legal rights.

> If an applicant believes the information is wrong, the applicant can inform the screening agency, which must verify the information and, if wrong, remove or correct the data, usually within 30 days.

> Applicants have the right to inspect their files.

Important Tips

> Just like your parents told you, honesty is the best policy. Fill out job applications truthfully. It's often not what they disclose, but the failure to disclose that costs applicants their dream job.

> Learn your rights under the Fair Credit Reporting Act. You can learn more by contacting the Federal Trade Commission at **www.ftc.gov**.

> Your state may also have specific laws or regulations governing background checks. Check with your state's Consumer Advocate or Attorney General's Office.

> Consider doing a background check on yourself. There is more information on how to do it in the next section. If you find inaccurate information, challenge it using the protections afforded to you under the FCRA.

Screening Yourself

It's important to check your own files and know what data exists about you. Making sure it is accurate and up to date will take away the angst you feel about the information and help you use it to your advantage.

For example, in a competitive job market, there can be thousands of resumes flooding in for one position. You might want to take the lead and do a background check on yourself, which you can then offer to a company. It might be one way to separate yourself from the pack. One way is to have a report compiled on yourself and made available to a potential employer.

> It is important to check your own files and know what data exists about you. Making sure it is accurate and up-to-date will take away the angst you feel about the information and help you use it to your advantage.

There is also the granddaddy of all information files: your FBI file. You can have access to this through the Freedom of Information Act (FOIA), which entitles you to request any record maintained by a federal executive branch agency. The agency must release the requested material unless it falls under one of nine exempt categories, like "national security," "privacy," or "confidential source."

To obtain your FBI file, you must write two letters — one to FBI head-quarters and one to the FBI field office closest to where you live. Address each letter to the FOIA office, and be sure to mark clearly on the envelope: "Attention — FOIA request." You may have to pay a slight fee: you are entitled to up to 100 pages of free copying and up to two hours of free research time, but you must pay for work that extends beyond those limits. There is no central office that processes FIOA requests; each government agency responds to requests for its own records.

According to the FBI, some single requests have resulted in processing thousands of pages of records. In the past 30 years, the FBI says it has handled over 300,000 requests and over six million pages of FBI documents have been released to the public. Your record may look kind of weird when you get it; an analyst will go over it to determine if any portions should be withheld, and will use a colored marker to delete any exempt material. Some of the most requested files (like Marilyn Monroe) and reports (like Roswell) are available online: **http://foia.fbi.gov/room.htm**.

Keep in mind: It can takes weeks or months for requests to be processed and there may not be a file on you.

 Important Tips

> Do a self check through ChoicePoint's ChoiceTrust.com (**www.choicetrust.com**). Or you can do a self check through Yahoo! Hot Jobs at **http://hotjobs.yahoo.com** and have the results shared with a prospective employer. You can also conduct a self check at **www.Americandatabank.net**.

> Type your own name into a variety of search engines, such as **www.google.com** or **www.dogpile.com**. You might be surprised at what comes up: old newspaper stories that mention you, birth and wedding announcements, your address and phone number. This won't provide much information from private records, but it will give you a flavor of the public information that prospective employers and others may find about you.

> If you want to check for files the federal government may have on you, but do not know which section of the Justice Department has the records

you are looking for, the Justice Management Division will forward your request to the section most likely to have it.

FOIA/PA Mail Referral Unit
Department of Justice
Room 114, LOC
Washington, D.C. 20530-0001

> Requests for Attorney General records should be addressed to:

Deputy Director
Office of Information and Privacy
Ste 570, Flag Building
Washington, D.C. 20530-0001

> Another useful tool is "Your Right to Federal Records," which is a joint publication of the General Services Administration and the Department of Justice. It is available for sale for one dollar per copy (Consumer Information Center, Department 320K, Pueblo, CO 81009) or it can be accessed at **www.usdoj.gov/04foia/04_7.html**.

 Let's Talk

These questions will help you, your family and others to begin a discussion about issues covered in this chapter.

1. Do we practice good safety rules for when workers are in our home?

2. Do we know if the service companies we use conduct criminal background checks on their employees who come into our home?

3. Do we know who can conduct a background check for us on a home job applicant? Do we know how to conduct a background check on someone we want to hire?

4. Do we know our rights if someone wants to conduct a background check on us when we apply for jobs? Do we know how to do background checks on ourselves?

CHAPTER 7: **Before Your House Is a Home**
Be Street Smart

Ardith Bugai is approaching 85. She is not known for stirring up trouble — she has lived on the family dairy farm, with its cattle and peach and cherry orchards, in quiet Elmwood Township, a small, rural community along the lakefront in Michigan. This is cherry country, with rolling hills dotted with woods. When her husband died, Bugai decided to sell 200 acres of the 500-acre farm because she was "getting old."[1]

But Bugai did not realize that the buyer planned to construct a housing development. And when Elmwood Township collectively realized that Stewart Investment Group planned to use 138 acres of that land for a 55-unit condominium development (named "Lincoln Meadows"), a battle erupted between the town government and zoning board and an enraged citizens' group. "The project," says Eric Saxon, a board member of Elmwood Citizens for Sensible Growth, "just doesn't fit into the neighborhood."

In the three years since developers first asked for township approval, Elmwood Citizens for Sensible Growth has twice sued the township to stop Lincoln Meadows, and a third lawsuit was filed over a zoning board of appeals ruling that could allow the construction despite the two previous court rulings. And for the third time, the 13th Circuit Court ruled in favor of Citizens for Sensible Growth.

Organizing the effort, says Saxon, would have been much tougher without the aid of the latest technology. Two seemingly simple items: e-mail and an organizational Web site, kept citizens interested and informed.

"It took some effort for people to learn about [the development plans]," he says. "Information is more readily available now. I see the Web as a place where the real nitty gritty of government can be published without a filter."

Know Your Neighborhood

Groups and individuals are now finding it much easier to go online to do their community due diligence. And new research provides additional insight into why it's important to do that research. For example, understanding why school testing results tie so closely to housing prices can help you avoid future financial trouble.

Elizabeth Warren, a professor at Harvard Law School, and her daughter, Amelia Warren Tyagi, a former McKinsey consultant, studied nearly 2,000 families that had gone bankrupt in the U.S. They analyzed federal data detailing what Americans actually spend their money on today compared to the 1970s.

The answer, found in their book *The Two Income Trap*, surprised them: most Americans are spending the bulk of their income on a mortgage on a house in a good school district. "Housing prices strongly mirror the perceived strength of the school district," Warren told an online magazine. "It's the only thing that fits the rest of the housing data. The houses haven't gotten much bigger. They're not newer. They don't have a whole lot more amenities. The average new house built in the U.S. is larger, but that's not what the median-income family is buying."[2]

If you are spending that much on a fixed expense like a mortgage you better understand as much as you can about your new neighborhood. According to Warren, a family today is "more likely to live in a house that's more than 25 years old — old wiring, old paint, old plumbing. Look at the studies of what a good school district yields in terms of prices: a 5-point increase on fourth-grade reading scores will translate into thousands of dollars in the value of a home in that school district, as opposed to the neighboring school district that didn't have the rise."

Educational statistics, safety and zoning information, resale and environmental data, and the all-important crime statistics on residential communities are available to the public. Since many of the most desirable homes fall in "good" school districts and are not the sparkling new homes, a home with a history can bring major problems with it that go beyond faulty plumbing.

Zoning classifications are the most important tool that a local government has to control the way that land is used in a community. Areas designated as residential may have further controls on housing density for single family homes, townhouses or multiple-family houses. There are usually areas set aside for industrial, commercial and recreational purposes.

Zoning boards spend their time listening to requests for exceptions to these rules or hearing arguments from parties who want to change or bend existing zoning regulations. And, these zoning decisions have a major impact on the surrounding neighborhoods. Citizens' groups increasingly get involved in testifying at hearings on proposals that could affect their property values or quality of life, and also help to create interest about issues in the local press.

Ever more cities and towns have Web sites that allow people to request zoning information. An example of an informative Web site is San Diego's site, **www.sannet.gov**. It includes a wide range of information, including times for garbage collection, crime statistics and the status of construction permits.

In Las Vegas, the Clark County School District has made things easier for this fast-growing area by loading zoning maps onto its Web site, **www.ccsd.net**; just type in your address and up pops your school zone and transportation information.

Did You Know?

- Educational statistics, safety and zoning information, resale and environmental data, and the all-important crime statistics on residential communities are available to the public.

- Zoning classifications are the most important tool that a local government has to control the way that land is used in a community.

- Many police departments post crime statistics for their city's neighborhoods on their Web sites.

In Northbrook, Illinois, a desirable neighborhood on the North Shore of Chicago, the city uses the Internet to inform its community on a variety of vital issues including zoning.

"I'm trying to get past where people have to go to legal notices in the newspaper and look for posted signs in lots," says Tom Poupard, Northbrook's director of community planning.

In a sense, posting zoning regulations, zoning maps and requests for zoning changes online, as more and more communities are doing, means citizens learn about plans for their community at a 21st century pace rather than an 18th century pace.

And it saves everyone money too. "Particularly with zoning regulations," Poupard says, "Developers feel they have to buy the book of new zoning standards, but in reality they only need a few pages, and by posting them on the Internet, it's saved the village lots of manpower time. We've saved money on printing costs, and we've saved developers and citizens the [$20] cost of buying the regulations."

Another example of a new use of the Internet is found at the Web site run by the city of Marietta in Georgia.

Citizens who go to **www.city.marietta.ga.us** can load any address in the Geographical Information System to learn who owns the property, how much they pay in property taxes and see an aerial photo of the lot and what surrounds it.

Real estate agents say another vital question home buyers often have deals with crime rates in neighborhoods they're considering. Do not rely on your perception of a neighborhood. Do some research.

Many police departments post crime statistics for their city's neighborhoods on their Web sites. There are also sites like Realtor.com, which will give you access to some crime statistics by zip code.

This was the information source that Anne Scott turned to after she had her van stolen from her driveway in St. Petersburg, Fla., a few years ago. She compared crime rates on **Realtor.com** and selected a new area to live in. She told her local newspaper, "I walk the dogs at night and I don't feel uncomfortable walking in the neighborhood after dark. I did in my old neighborhood."[3]

Important Tips

> Contact your municipal, county and state government, and school district (or those of the places where you think you might move). Find out what housing, zoning, educational, crime and fire statistics they post.

> More and more communities are posting new information on the Internet daily. It's much less time-consuming to go online than to go to the courthouse digging through paper.

> Look at the zoning and planning maps for your community. Just because quiet woods surround your house doesn't mean it will stay that way. Zoning information will at least alert you to what MIGHT be built next door.

> Find out if there is a local citizens group in your community. They will likely maintain a Web site full of useful information on the area.

> Get to know your elected and appointed officials. No technology replaces personal relationships.

> **www.realtor.com** provides detailed education, demographic and socio-economic data, as well as some crime statistics by zip code and the group's take on real estate market conditions across the nation.

> Check Globexplorer (**www.globexplorer.com**) to actually see a satellite view of your new home and neighborhood.

Know Your House

There is more information available out there that will help you learn about your home, or potential home, than ever before. The most recent addition to your arsenal — the insurance claims history report.

That dream home you purchased and moved into might have a dark past — not in the "Amityville Horror" sense, but when you contact an insurance company for that all-important homeowner's policy, you might find out some ugly things. For instance, the previous owner may have had multiple claims against it — for water damage, mold, theft. Because it can be very expensive to repair and insure that home, an insurance company may be very reluctant to insure the house for a new owner.

Did You Know?

- Insurance carriers have relied on claims history reports for more than ten years to help them decide if a home is insurable under their criteria and at what cost. Consumers have always had access, too, but it was a slow process. Now home buyers and sellers can get instant access to the information online.

Insurance carriers have relied on claims history reports for more than ten years to help them decide if a home is insurable under their criteria and at what cost. Consumers have always had access, too, but it was a slow process. Now home buyers and sellers can get instant access to the information online.

Keep in mind a claims history report is not the same as the standard real estate disclosure form you may be familiar with and may contain information you won't find on the real estate disclosure form. For example, it may show a history of vandalism or theft. It can also serve as a road map for your pre-purchase home inspector to ensure past damage has been properly repaired.

Cindy Kaul, principle broker at Colonnade Realty in Virginia, provides an example on her excellent agency Web site **(www.colonnaderealty.com)**. "I was representing a beautiful waterfront home at Lake Monticello. The owners had maintained their home extremely well. It sold quickly and we anticipated a smooth closing. However, when the buyer went to get their Homeowner's policy, the new company ran a check on the property and found that a claim had been filed a few years ago for a water leak resulting in a payment to the owner of several thousand dollars."

"They denied the new owner coverage stating that they were afraid because of the extent of the damage (assumed from the amount paid) that there might be mold issues. When I questioned the seller, I found out what really happened. While the seller was out of town a pipe broke and caused some water to enter the house. A neighbor noticed the situation immediately and called a plumber who quickly made a repair. The actual plumbing repair cost less than $200, but the water damaged a piece of antique furniture and that was the reason for the higher claim. It had nothing to do with large amounts of damage or water."

Ms. Kaul's example is an excellent illustration of why extra diligence is required. If there had been no insurance claims history report created as part of the sale, the new homeowners might not have learned of the previous water damage. If it had been major damage, not knowing could have led to severe problems down the road if mold or wood damage appeared.

Likewise, getting a copy of the insurance history of the home gave the new owners the information needed to ask the right questions: Has the home been damaged by water and, if so, how badly?

No less a person than Founding Father James Madison believed that "knowledge will forever govern ignorance, and a people who mean to be their own Governors must arm themselves with the power knowledge gives." Here are some ways to arm yourself with that knowledge as you make one of the most important decisions of your life — where to buy that house of your dreams.

Important Tips

> Obtain a claims history report before you buy or sell a house. There are only two homeowner's insurance claims history products today: ChoicePoint's Comprehensive Loss Underwriting Exchange or C.L.U.E.® report and the Insurance Services Organization's A-Plus report. You can purchase your C.L.U.E. report online at **www.choicetrust.com** or by calling **1-866-527-2600**. You can get your A-Plus report by calling **1-800-709-8842**. Only the owner of a home may request a copy of a claims history report before a contract is signed on the property.

> If you are a seller in a particularly competitive real estate market (like New York City or San Francisco) where sellers usually get offers right away, provide a copy of your report to your Real Estate agent to share with prospective buyers.

> If you are a buyer, request a copy of a C.L.U.E. report at **www.choicetrust.com**. The seller will be contacted to give permission for you to view the claims history of the property you want to buy. If you don't have online access, ask your Real Estate agent to request a copy.

> Ask your insurance company how they view the filing of claims and how that affects your premium. Each carrier has unique criteria for determining how much to charge you for insurance and each company views claims differently.

> If you don't have an insurance agent yet, check out your state's insurance department Web site or contact the Insurance Information Institute (**www.iii.org**) to learn what unique laws or regulations are placed on insurance companies in your state.

> If you have a homeowners claim and you're concerned it may impact your ability to sell your home, take advantage of the Fair Credit Reporting Act. It gives you the right to place a statement in the file that explains your side of the story.

 Let's Talk

These questions will help you, your family and others to begin a discussion about issues covered in this chapter.

1. Do we know what information is available from our local government about our house, our neighborhood, our community and our schools?

2. How does our local government post news about community improvement and proposed projects that could impact our home or neighborhood?

3. Who are our elected representatives for our neighborhood at the city and county government level? Who represents us in the state legislature and U.S. Congress? Do we know how to contact them if we need them?

4. Have we asked for a claims history report on a house we want to buy?

5. Have we checked our own report to help sell our current home or just to ensure it is accurate?

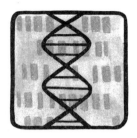

CHAPTER 8: **DNA Testing**

Who Are You?

We all know that television series often drive pop culture and define what's hot and what's not. Right now, it's very hot to be a criminologist thanks to the number one rated television program — CBS Television's *CSI: Crime Scene Investigation*. CSI has helped make "buccal swabs" and "gun shot residue" common language around the office water cooler. In other words, DNA is chic.

Deoxyribose Nucleic Acid or DNA is a star performer right now on and off screen. Because each human being's DNA is unique, it is the ultimate identifier. Real CSIs, police officers and forensic investigators, rely on DNA to help free the innocent and convict the guilty. It is arguably the greatest crime fighting tool since the use of fingerprints became common more than 100 years ago. In fact DNA is the fingerprint of this century.

By and large, there haven't been many occasions for an individual to come into contact with DNA in a meaningful way. That is, until very recently. In this chapter, we'll explore ways DNA can be useful to you now and perhaps in the future.

What Is DNA?

In simple terms, DNA is the blueprint for all life — every cell in your body contains DNA that is unique to you. No one else in the world has the same DNA you do, even if you have an identical twin.

Not all DNA is used for the same purpose, though. Some DNA markers are indicators of possible health issues.

And, contrary to what you may have seen on television or read in a book, the DNA used to identify a person is not a treasure trove of biological information that can be used against you. The DNA markers that identify you (like what you see each week on *CSI*) has no purpose other than identification. We call that iDNA, for "identification DNA," which translates into a unique set of 26 numbers that is "you."

Remember, iDNA can't tell you why you crave pizza or refuse to eat your veggies. It can't tell you if you are likely to develop a particular disease in the future. But, iDNA can help you prove you are who you claim to be. And more.

DNA and Your Ancestors

One of the ways you can put the power of DNA to work for you is to learn more about your family history. Not just a few generations back in time. DNA can take you back centuries.

Take, for instance, the thousands of African Americans who are now using DNA technology to track their genealogy. About 12 million slaves were brought to the New World after 1600, and it is possible to use a

DNA test kit to begin accurately mapping a family tree. Tina Dunkley of Decatur, Georgia, asked her 89-year-old mother to swab the inside of her cheek, and then she sent the sample in to African-Ancestry, Inc. A few weeks later, Dunkley learned that her mother's DNA matched the DNA of the Temne people in modern Sierra Leone, in western Africa.[1]

"It was wonderful, sacred information, a spiritual experience," the art gallery director told the *Atlanta Journal-Constitution*.

DNA used in this way provides a direct link to a family's history in a way traditional research methods never could. It puts a human face on a very powerful technology.

Important Tips

> Genealogical research can be done by companies like African-Ancestry Inc., **www.africanancestry.com, 1-202-439-0641,** and Family Tree DNA, **www.familytreedna.com** (Fees vary and can exceed $600).

> DNA Prints Genomics charges a minimum of $158 to analyze the DNA of people who want to know more about their roots: **www.dnaprint.com 1-941-366-3400**.

> For more general information on tracing your family history, two good places to start are the Ellis Island Foundation, **www.ellisisland.org,** and **www.ancestry.com**, which accesses several different databases, some of which charge a fee.

DNA and Your Health

DNA testing may be the hottest new tool in genealogy, but it is in the area of medical testing that it will likely provide a more direct benefit.

For more than 50 years now, scientists have been studying DNA. Researchers, who spent the past 15 years working to map the entire genetic code of humans, are now beginning to look for ways to use the information to develop tests and medicines to predict, treat and prevent diseases using medical DNA. (You can learn more about the Human Genome Project on a variety of Web sites.)

Each year, new tests that use medical DNA are developed that can help identify individuals with propensities towards specific ailments. For instance, some tests are used to discover whether a patient might be predisposed to heart disease or certain types of cancer. Still other tests find whether parents are likely to pass along diseases and disorders to their children, diseases such as cystic fibrosis, sickle cell anemia and Tay-Sachs disease. This is valuable information that a new or prospective parent may (or may not) want to know.

The use of DNA to predict the likelihood of a person developing a disease is not without controversy. Some people fear the results of medical genetics could lead to a new form of discrimination where people with certain genetic profiles become uninsurable. If that were to occur, it would be a monumental misuse of a powerful medical test.

> The use of DNA to predict the likelihood of a person developing a disease is not without controversy. Some people fear the results of medical genetics could lead to a new form of discrimination where people with certain genetic profiles become uninsurable.

Then there is the emotional element of medical genetic testing to consider. Do you really want to know about the *potential* for contracting a debilitating illness? The stress of worrying about an illness that may never come could be a problem in and of itself.

For example, you may never display a single symptom of heart disease if you eat properly, exercise and avoid smoking. But then again, you may not be motivated enough to adopt a healthy lifestyle without the knowledge you are predisposed to the disease.

The complexities of medical genetic testing make it vitally important that you discuss these issues with your family and personal physician. They can advise you as to what, if any, benefits there would be to you as well as outline the physical and emotional risks to you. Then, most importantly, you can make an informed decision because you will have taken personal responsibility for learning about the consequences — good and bad — of the tests.

Important Tips

> Learn more about the Human Genome Project and the many exciting potential technologies and treatments that are now being researched. Visit **www.doegenomes.org** for more information. Or search "Human Genome Project" using your favorite search engine.

> New genetic tests are constantly being introduced to address common and rare diseases and disorders. Ask your doctor if you should be tested and for what disease.

> There are hundreds of Web sites that describe the up and down sides of medical genetic testing. Sites like **www.webmd.com** offer general information that will help you prepare for the discussion with your doctor. You can also find more information about genetic testing for your children at **www.kidshealth.org**.

- Each year, new tests that use medical DNA are developed that can help identify individuals with propensities towards specific ailments.

DNA and Your Child's Safety

There is no good way to say to a parent, "iDNA is something that may help if your child is kidnapped or killed." It's too horrible to think about. But a kidnapper is as much a terrorist as Osama bin Laden. There's nothing but sheer terror involved in child abductions. But as helpless as you feel, there is something you can do.

Chapter Five included a series of items you should collect to create a child identification kit at home. Now, I want you to include one more item — an iDNA sample.

Remember the fingerprint of this century is iDNA. It can be invaluable in helping to identify children who are too young to speak or have been missing for so long, they no longer remember who they are. In 2003 iDNA was used to prove the identities of two pre-teen children kidnapped as toddlers. Tragically for the still grieving families, the children were not theirs. Yet, the incredible power of DNA was proven once again.

Important Tips

> Companies and non-profit organizations offer kits to parents, with the promise that their child's iDNA is not stored in any databases. Parents themselves can store the iDNA sample, and it may last for up to 80 years. Kits differ in quality and cost, so do your homework before you invest in a kit.

You can purchase home iDNA kits from the following companies:

- CatGee: **www.catgee.com**.
- Code Amber: **www.codeamber.org**.
- DNA Life Print: **www.dna-lifeprint.com**.
- DNA Testing Center: **www.dnatestingcentre.com**.

- Fingerprint America:
  www.fingerprintamerica.com.
- KiddieID.com: **www.kiddieid/idkids.com**.
- My Precious Kid:
  www.mypreciouskid.com.

DNA and Victims of Crime

Thanks to *CSI* and other television shows, news programs and movies, the power of DNA to help convict the guilty and free the innocent is well known.

What is less well known is the growing backlog of DNA evidence collected at crime scenes that sits on police department shelves, gathering dust. The US Department of Justice estimates nearly a half million sexual assault evidence kits have never been processed for lack of funding. If processed, conservative estimates project tens of thousands of crimes could be solved and other crimes prevented (sexual offenders commit an average of 9-12 crimes before they are caught).

Every state has a law permitting law enforcement officials to create a database of convicted felons to aid in solving crimes. There is a federal DNA database of known felons, too, referred to as CODIS for "Combined DNA Index System."

The concept is simple; if a person gets out of prison and commits another crime, iDNA on file can be matched against the evidence collected at the crime scene, just like on TV. But the crime scene evidence must be processed and the state must have created an iDNA database of known criminals for the system to work. And, the state must upload the iDNA information to the federal database.

Congress has been struggling with this issue for several years, prompted in part by the story of Debbie Smith, a Virginia woman who was raped in her own home. Her assailant was eventually caught when the iDNA of a convicted felon matched the crime scene evidence from Debbie Smith's attack — six years after the incident.

Since that time, Smith has become a tireless victims right's advocate and forceful proponent for the use of iDNA.

"I didn't realize how powerful DNA is. I don't think everyone realizes how powerful it is," advises Smith. "Anytime a great tool such as DNA is available, yet not used, society commits a crime against its members."

Important Tips

> If you are the victim of a violent crime, insist any DNA evidence collected at the crime scene be immediately processed and compared against your state's DNA database (if they have one) and the federal CODIS system. You can find out more about CODIS at **www.fbi.gov/hq/lab/codis/index1.htm**.

> RAINN — the Rape, Abuse, & Incest National Network — operates a Web site and hotline for victims of sexual assault, including advocacy and counseling services. To learn more visit **www.rainn.org** or call **1-800-656-4673 (HOPE)**.

> The National Center for Victims of Crime is also an excellent resource. Call **1-800-211-7996** or visit **www.ncvc.org** for more information.

> Lifetime Television is spearheading an effort to increase funding to help reduce the backlog of sexual assault evidence with a goal of putting more rapists behind bars. Visit **www.lifetimeTV.com/community** to learn more and sign a petition calling for Congressional action. If you wish to make a tax deductible contribution to help fund DNA testing of sexual assault evidence, visit **www.rapeevidence.org**.

Let's Talk

These questions will help you, your family and others to begin a discussion about issues covered in this chapter.

1. How can DNA be useful for our family?

2. Do any members of our family have a history of diseases or disorders that can be detected by medical DNA tests? Have we discussed with each other and our family doctor the benefits of medical DNA tests?

3. Have we added an iDNA sample to our home ID kit?

4. Does our state have a DNA database of convicted felons? Does our state have a backlog of unprocessed DNA evidence that could help solve crimes? What can we do to help reduce any backlog?

CHAPTER 9: **Privacy and Security**

Information for a Safer America

In this book, I've tried to show how technology can help manage the ever increasing pace of change of our lives. I've provided some very practical information and sources of where you can find even more assistance. But, I've also tried to challenge you — albeit in a subtle way — to think about how information tools and technology should be used to protect you and your family.

There is a growing call for a national discussion about what information is legitimate for use, how this information should be accessed, and by whom. That's a very healthy discussion — one which I ultimately hope you will join — but let me encourage you to first master the three Gs: Get Aware, Get Informed and then, Get Involved.

Get Aware of the Risks You Face

One of the great themes of recent Hollywood movies has been the perils of progress. Movies about man *versus* machine — from the Terminator series to the Matrix Trilogy — ask the question, "Can we handle all the technological advances or will we somehow make our lives obsolete, not easier?"

It does make for great cinema, but the reality isn't nearly as dark and sinister as it appears on the big screen.

While we can't just stuff the technology genie back into the bottle, no matter how badly some people want to, we can responsibly harness the incredible power of information and technology for the good of society. But first, it will require you to "get aware" of the risks around you and your family and your new responsibilities in a changing world. Acting like an ostrich by sticking our heads in the sand no longer works. The risks we thought could not reach us are now at our doorstep.

We've covered some of the everyday risks you face today in this book. We've explored ways to avoid the financial risks of making a bad home purchase decision. The same for avoiding the physical dangers of allowing a perfect stranger into your home. We've highlighted the emotional risks to your children inherent in allowing them to wander around the Internet unsupervised — something you would never do if the streets were real, not cyber.

Take the time to identify what other risks exist in your life and take the responsibility for acting to reduce them.

But risk is a moving target. Think about how our world has changed in your lifetime. The America of 2004 is not the same as fifty years ago, when a neighbor's recommendation was a good as gold. Cops provided security just by walking a beat. No one needed to question your identity because your driver's license had your name printed on it in black and white. (And it was real, not a near perfect imitation bought over the Internet.)

Times have changed and so have the roles of institutions we traditionally relied on to look out for us. Police officers now solves crimes, not prevent them. Today, prevention becomes the job of business owners and neighborhood crime watch groups. No longer can the government tell us if a doctor, plumber or nursing home are good just by issuing a license. It's our job now to ask the questions that will help us make better decisions to improve our peace of mind and way of life.

Bottom line — it's the responsibility of every one of us to become aware and stay aware of the risks in our daily lives, even as the risks themselves change.

Get Informed About the Root Causes of Risk

You might not expect me to acknowledge this next statement, but it is true: technology and information can only solve so many of our problems. In many cases, they are only stop-gap measures that temporarily slow the steadily increasing risks around us. Risk can only be reduced so far using these tools before you have to get to the root cause of the underlying risk.

Only if we, as a society, take the steps to become more informed about what is causing our world to become riskier, can we truly make the world a safer, more secure place to live. The place to start is with you and your family.

Let me give you two examples.

Remember what it was like, before the business scandals of the past few years? We trusted companies to wisely invest our 401K plans. We often blindly bought stocks and we believed the reassuring e-mails from our brokers and the people in charge. The warning signs were all there that something might be out of control, but we ignored the alerts.

Technology — and for that matter more rules and regulations — could not have prevented smart, but unethical people from the actions they took. More due diligence by us could have led to a different outcome.

Likewise, remember what it was like, before 9/11? We boarded passenger airplanes without thinking much about how those planes could be hijacked, let alone driven into buildings. We did not consider (or we ignored) the violence and hatred building for us in many parts of the world.

While technology and information could have prevented the 19 hijackers from boarding airplanes on 9/11, it could not address the root cause of the desire to crash the planes into the heart of America.

Well informed people, however, can.

Take the time to look beyond the fact that risk exists, and find out why it exists. If you're worried about crime, learn more about the causes of crime in your community and what you can do to help reduce those root causes.

 Did You Know?

- Times have changed and so have the roles of institutions we traditionally relied on to look out for us. Police officers now solves crimes, not prevent them.

- Bottom line — it's the responsibility of every one of us to become aware and stay aware of the risks in our daily lives, even as the risks themselves change.

- Only if we, as a society, take the steps to become more informed about what is causing our world to become riskier, can we truly make the world a safer, more secure place to live. The place to start is with you and your family.

- If you're worried about crime, learn more about the causes of crime in your community and what you can do to help reduce those root causes.

Often times, looking beyond the walls of your own life means looking at how the rest of the world lives. Understand the differences between cultures and celebrate the diversity. Help your children to look and understand, too.

A 2002 Roper study for the National Geographic Society found that only 15 percent of young American adults (18 to 24 years) could find Iraq on a map. Seventeen percent could find Afghanistan. Amazingly, 11 percent could not even find the US on the map.

You and your children can start to gain a better understanding of the root causes of anti-Americanism by viewing the world through the eyes of a newspaper reader in other countries. (It will also help improve geographic literacy, too.) One excellent Web site that will link you to newspapers, magazines and even television stations around the world is **www.newslink.org**, operated by The American Journalism Review. This is a great way to be informed about other perspectives of our country, and, where appropriate, learn the "whys" in this troubled world. You don't have to believe the criticisms of our country, but you should know about them.

You can also learn more about the great religions and cultures that shape other societies. Use any of the major search engines to unlock the wealth of knowledge that is on the Internet and available for the asking.

Here in the United States, we never really had to worry about understanding the rest of the world. Now, not knowing about the rest of the world has the potential to affect you directly.

Get Involved in the Discussion

You're aware of risk. You're informed about the nature of risk and the root causes of it. Now, it's time to get involved by using the tools and resources outlined in the previous chapters to give yourself more peace of mind. To restore some of the trust and faith lost during the past few years.

Technology and information tools can be used for doing good — solving and even preventing crimes; protecting your hard earned money; helping to find that special someone; and the list goes on and on. Yet, misused, these same tools can be harmful to an individual or society at large by invading the privacy of innocent people or, worse, creating new risks.

Earlier in this chapter, I said we, as a country, need to have a discussion about what sort of rules we want to create that promote the positive benefits of information, and punish the misuse of the technology that can help keep us safe.

There is a fine line we must be careful not to cross in either direction. If your personal data is misused, has the world been made safer for you? No. At the same time, people have to stand up and say, for instance, "If we don't use DNA technology to fight rape, then we're putting women at risk."

Ground Rules

These are issues that are best addressed by society as a whole, engaged in a dialogue with certain ground rules:

> The discussion should be based on a real risk, not a hypothetical or "what if" scenario.

> The discussion should be passionate, but not emotional. Baseless claims without fact only make for bad policy. We need to stick to the facts, but defend our positions with vigor.

> We should talk about the use of information, not the availability. Information exists and it can be used for good and bad. The way to ensure it is used for the good of society is to set strict rules for when information can be used, by whom and for what purpose. Strict penalties for violating the rules should also come into play. Today, we have few, if any, of either.

> We should agree that the best framework for using information is one where people give their consent to the collection *and* use of information, understanding that law enforcement and national security needs may outweigh the ability to get permission on a rare basis. And when you do give permission, your data should not be used for a different purpose unless you're asked again for permission to use the information in a different way.

> Everyone should have the right (and ability) to see what information exists about them, irrespective of the type, source or use of the information. In others words, expand the principles of the existing Fair Credit Reporting Act to all types of information: the right to access, the right to question accuracy (causing a prompt investigation), and the right to comment if a negative record is found to be accurate.

Did You Know?

- Empowering technology for good, punishing those who use it for bad — that is, hopefully, our future.

- While our world may be riskier today, we have more and better information weapons to defend us at our disposal than ever before.

- To learn more about the responsible use of information visit www.choicepoint.com.

Over the past several years, one of the nation's leading privacy experts — Dr. Alan F. Westin — has studied attitudes about privacy. He says about 30 percent of us are "privacy fundamentalists" who, regardless of risk and safeguards, don't want personal information shared under any circumstances or we're the "privacy unconcerned," individuals who don't care about or are willing to overlook privacy incursions.

The rest of us — the other 70 percent of America — are "privacy pragmatists." We want a balance between privacy *and* risk reduction.

Empowering technology for good, punishing those who use it for bad — that is, hopefully, our future. An informed dialogue about these issues, played out in public, is how that future will happen. I urge you to join in the discussion, hopefully as a privacy pragmatist, when the time comes.

The potential for using information tools for good is as exciting as it is boundless. While our world may be riskier today, we have more and better information weapons to defend us at our disposal than ever before. Arm yourself, inform yourself and use what you have learned in this book to create a safer, more secure life for yourself and loved ones.

Let's Talk

These questions will help you, your family and others to begin a discussion about issues covered in this chapter.

1. How are we at risk in our daily lives?

2. What steps can we take to reduce or eliminate those risks?

3. What are we doing to learn why risks exist?

4. How well do we know what is happening in our own community, country and the world? What can we do to increase our awareness and knowledge?

5. How do we view personal privacy?

Sources

Chapter 1

1. Gartner Inc. Research report July 2003 for period July 2002-June 2003.

2. Robert O'Harrow Jr., "Identity Crisis," *The Washington Post Magazine*, August 10, 2003.

3. Jack Hitt, "Confessions of a Spam King," *The New York Times Magazine*, September 28, 2003.

4. Robert O'Harrow Jr., "Identity Crisis," *The Washington Post Magazine*, August 10, 2003.

Chapter 2

1. Jack Hitt, "Confessions of a Spam King," *The New York Times Magazine*, September 28, 2003.

2. The Associated Press, Chicago Bureau. October 30, 2003.

3. Report from the U.S Energy Department Computer Incident Advisory Capability Department. October 2003.

4. John Schwartz, "Snoop Software Power Raises Privacy Concerns," *The New York Times,* October 10, 2003.

5. CBSnews.com, "Are you being snooped?" October 10, 2003.

6. CBSnews.com, "Are you being snooped?" October 10, 2003.

7. Washingtonpost.com chat. October 9, 2003.

8. Op-ed by Sam Brownback, "Who Will Police the Pirate Hunters?," *The Wall Street Journal*, October 7, 2003.

Chapter 3

1. James L. McQuivey, Forrester Technographics, "RIP: The Online Consumer."

2. www.fbi.gov.

3. Beth Cox, "Hijacking and Fraud Plague Ebay Users," www.internetnews.com, October 11, 2002.

4. Beth Cox, "And the Online Fraud Goes On," www.internetnews.com, February 14, 2003.

Chapter 4

1. Frank Davies, "Disease Database Gets Broad Backing," *The Miami Herald*, October 23, 2003.
2. The Rand Corporation, "Evaluating the Feasibility of Developing National Outcomes Databases," Study from May 2003.
3. John Webster Web site, www.homepages.dsu.edu/websterj.
4. Public Citizen Web site, www.citizen.org.
5. Robert Forman, University of Pennsylvania, August 2003.
6. Gannett News Service, "Rating America's Nursing Homes," Special Report, www.content.gannettonline.com, 2003.

Chapter 5

1. National Center for Missing and Exploited Children, "Online Victimization" Report, June 2000.
2. The Oprah Winfrey Show, "Child Stalkers Online," February 7, 2002.
3. Cheryl Wetzstein, "Porn on the Web Exploding," *The Washington Times*, October 9, 2003.
4. Diane Rado, "Teachers Can Hide Criminal Records," *The Chicago Tribune*, November 30, 2003.

Chapter 7

1. Stacey Smith, "Woman Unaware of Condo Plan," *The Traverse City Record-Eagle*, May 28, 2002.
2. Katherine Mieszkowski, "Americans Are Not Going Broke over Lattes," October 13, 2003.
3. Janet Zink, "Crime Rates Factor in Homebuyer Selection," *The St. Petersburg Times*, May 17, 2002.

Chapter 8

1. Bill Hendrick, "Putting the Gene in Genealogy," *The Atlanta-Journal Constitution*. December 14, 2003.